OPPOSING
VIEWPOINTS®
SERIES

| Corporate Farming

Other Books of Related Interest

Opposing Viewpoints Series

Agricultural Subsidies
Genetic Engineering
Global Sustainability
Globalization
Nutrition

At Issue Series

Food Insecurity
Genetically Modified Food
Organic Food
Superfoods
The Local Food Movement

Current Controversies Series

Conserving the Environment
Factory Farming
Food
Pesticides
The Global Food Crisis

"Congress shall make no law … abridging the freedom of speech, or of the press."

First Amendment to the US Constitution

The basic foundation of our democracy is the First Amendment guarantee of freedom of expression. The Opposing Viewpoints series is dedicated to the concept of this basic freedom and the idea that it is more important to practice it than to enshrine it.

OPPOSING VIEWPOINTS® SERIES

| Corporate Farming

Avery Elizabeth Hurt, Book Editor

GREENHAVEN PUBLISHING

Published in 2018 by Greenhaven Publishing, LLC
353 3rd Avenue, Suite 255, New York, NY 10010

Articles in Greenhaven Publishing anthologies are often edited for length to meet page
requirements. In addition, original titles of these works are changed to clearly present
the main thesis and to explicitly indicate the author's opinion. Every effort is made to
ensure that Greenhaven Publishing accurately reflects the original intent of the authors.
Every effort has been made to trace the owners of the copyrighted material.

Cover image: Evgenii Sribnyi/Shutterstock.com

Library of Congress Cataloging-in-Publication Data

Names: Hurt, Avery Elizabeth, editor.
Title: Corporate farming / Avery Elizabeth Hurt, editor.
Description: New York : Greenhaven Publishing, [2018] | Series: Opposing viewpoints
| Audience: Grade 9 to 12. | Includes bibliographical references and index.
Identifiers: LCCN 2017004979| ISBN 9781534500518 (library bound) |
  ISBN 9781534500495 (pbk.)
Subjects: LCSH: Farm corporations--Juvenile literature. | Agricultural
  industries--Juvenile literature. | Organic farming--Juvenile literature.
Classification: LCC HD1714 .C67 2017 | DDC 338.1--dc23
LC record available at https://lccn.loc.gov/2017004979

Manufactured in the United States of America

Website: http://greenhavenpublishing.com

Contents

Chapter 3: Is Corporate Farming Economically Sustainable?

Chapter 4: Is Corporate Farming Morally Justifiable?

The Importance of Opposing Viewpoints

Perhaps every generation experiences a period in time in which the populace seems especially polarized, starkly divided on the important issues of the day and gravitating toward the far ends of the political spectrum and away from a consensus-facilitating middle ground. The world that today's students are growing up in and that they will soon enter into as active and engaged citizens is deeply fragmented in just this way. Issues relating to terrorism, immigration, women's rights, minority rights, race relations, health care, taxation, wealth and poverty, the environment, policing, military intervention, the proper role of government—in some ways, perennial issues that are freshly and uniquely urgent and vital with each new generation—are currently roiling the world.

If we are to foster a knowledgeable, responsible, active, and engaged citizenry among today's youth, we must provide them with the intellectual, interpretive, and critical-thinking tools and experience necessary to make sense of the world around them and of the all-important debates and arguments that inform it. After all, the outcome of these debates will in large measure determine the future course, prospects, and outcomes of the world and its peoples, particularly its youth. If they are to become successful members of society and productive and informed citizens, students need to learn how to evaluate the strengths and weaknesses of someone else's arguments, how to sift fact from opinion and fallacy, and how to test the relative merits and validity of their own opinions against the known facts and the best possible available information. The landmark series Opposing Viewpoints has been providing students with just such critical-thinking skills and exposure to the debates surrounding society's most urgent contemporary issues for many years, and it continues to serve this essential role with undiminished commitment, care, and rigor.

The key to the series's success in achieving its goal of sharpening students' critical-thinking and analytic skills resides in its title—

Opposing Viewpoints. In every intriguing, compelling, and engaging volume of this series, readers are presented with the widest possible spectrum of distinct viewpoints, expert opinions, and informed argumentation and commentary, supplied by some of today's leading academics, thinkers, analysts, politicians, policy makers, economists, activists, change agents, and advocates. Every opinion and argument anthologized here is presented objectively and accorded respect. There is no editorializing in any introductory text or in the arrangement and order of the pieces. No piece is included as a "straw man," an easy ideological target for cheap point-scoring. As wide and inclusive a range of viewpoints as possible is offered, with no privileging of one particular political ideology or cultural perspective over another. It is left to each individual reader to evaluate the relative merits of each argument— as he or she sees it, and with the use of ever-growing critical-thinking skills—and grapple with his or her own assumptions, beliefs, and perspectives to determine how convincing or successful any given argument is and how the reader's own stance on the issue may be modified or altered in response to it.

This process is facilitated and supported by volume, chapter, and selection introductions that provide readers with the essential context they need to begin engaging with the spotlighted issues, with the debates surrounding them, and with their own perhaps shifting or nascent opinions on them. In addition, guided reading and discussion questions encourage readers to determine the authors' point of view and purpose, interrogate and analyze the various arguments and their rhetoric and structure, evaluate the arguments' strengths and weaknesses, test their claims against available facts and evidence, judge the validity of the reasoning, and bring into clearer, sharper focus the reader's own beliefs and conclusions and how they may differ from or align with those in the collection or those of their classmates.

Research has shown that reading comprehension skills improve dramatically when students are provided with compelling, intriguing, and relevant "discussable" texts. The subject matter of these collections could not be more compelling, intriguing, or urgently relevant to today's students and the world they are poised to inherit. The anthologized articles and the reading and discussion questions that are included with them also provide the basis for stimulating, lively, and passionate classroom debates. Students who are compelled to anticipate objections to their own argument and identify the flaws in those of an opponent read more carefully, think more critically, and steep themselves in relevant context, facts, and information more thoroughly. In short, using discussable text of the kind provided by every single volume in the Opposing Viewpoints series encourages close reading, facilitates reading comprehension, fosters research, strengthens critical thinking, and greatly enlivens and energizes classroom discussion and participation. The entire learning process is deepened, extended, and strengthened.

For all of these reasons, Opposing Viewpoints continues to be exactly the right resource at exactly the right time—when we most need to provide readers with the critical-thinking tools and skills that will not only serve them well in school but also in their careers and their daily lives as decision-making family members, community members, and citizens. This series encourages respectful engagement with and analysis of opposing viewpoints and fosters a resulting increase in the strength and rigor of one's own opinions and stances. As such, it helps make readers "future ready," and that readiness will pay rich dividends for the readers themselves, for the citizenry, for our society, and for the world at large.

Introduction

For many people, the word "farming" brings up images of a man in overalls bending over rows of vegetables, a woman perched on a three-legged stool milking cows, or perhaps children on the back of a pick-up truck, helping their parents get in the hay before those purple clouds on the horizon bring rain. Of course we all know that nowadays Old MacDonald is more likely to be driving a combine than wielding a hoe, and cows are milked by machines. But what may not be so obvious is that the farms that grow our food have become enormous, industrial operations. This doesn't mean there are no small family farms left. According to a 2012 census taken by the United States Department of Agriculture (USDA), 97 percent of US farms are family farms, and 88 percent are small family farms. But even though 88 percent of farms are officially "small," that doesn't mean that 88 percent of the nation's food supply is being grown by small farms. According to research conducted by the Pew Charitable Trust, in 2002 the average US hog farm produced a little over 2,000 animals. But averages can be deceiving. That same year, the majority of the hogs produced came from operations ten times that size. Similar figures apply to chicken and cattle farms. That 12 percent of farms is doing the lion's share of the farming.

Most of these operations raise only one type of animal and often specialize in only one phase of the animal's life. Corn, wheat, and rice are also grown on huge farms that plant only one crop. In addition, many small family farms grow produce and animals for larger operations, such as Tyson chicken. Most of the food we eat passes through a large corporation somewhere along the way to the table, even if it didn't start there.

Industrial farming relies heavily on chemical inputs such as fertilizers, herbicides, and pesticides—and for the animals, antibiotics. Fertilizers are needed because growing only one crop again and again on the same land depletes the soil of nutrients;

pesticides and herbicides are needed because single crop fields attract the insects and weeds that thrive with and on those crops. Animals that are kept confined in close quarters with other animals are much more likely to get sick, so keeping them healthy requires a liberal use of antibiotics. The wisdom of this approach to farming is raising serious questions about the safety of our food supply and the risks to the environment.

The consolidation of the farming industry into the hands of a few extremely large operations raises economic concerns as well. Is such a system fair? Or are large corporations edging out small farmers and denying them a means of livelihood? Is consolidating the food system into the control of a few corporations even economically sustainable?

As the world population continues to grow, the question of how we will feed everyone is becoming more and more urgent. Some argue that corporate industrial farming is the only way to feed the world. Others argue that not only is large-scale industrial farming unnecessary, it's dangerous.

The questions are complex, and no simple answers will suffice. Even people who agree that large-scale industrial farming is not the best approach are not always in agreement about what alternative is both better and workable. Food is one of our most basic needs, and questions about what we eat, where it comes from, and how it is processed and distributed can create a lot of passion. *Opposing Viewpoints: Corporate Farming* tackles controversies surrounding twenty-first century farming in chapters titled "Can We Feed the World Without Corporate Farms?" "Is Corporate Farming Environmentally Sustainable?" "Is Corporate Farming Economically Sustainable?" and "Is Corporate Farming Morally Justifiable?" You will read diverse points of view discussing many aspects of these issues. You may not come away with any firm answers on any given issue, but you will certainly have a more nuanced look at the questions being debated. And you may come away with some ideas of your own for how to improve the food system.

CHAPTER 1

Can We Feed the World Without Corporate Farms?

Chapter Preface

By 2050, experts estimate that the world population will reach almost 10 billion people. Feeding that many people will be a challenge, and not one we can wait much longer to address.

Of course the world already has a hunger problem. According to the United Nations, about one in nine people do not get enough food to live a healthy life. The majority of the underfed, two-thirds, live in Asia. However, the highest *percentage* of hungry people is in sub-Saharan Africa, where one person in four is undernourished. Despite the epidemics of obesity, diabetes, and other ills created by over-eating in developed nations, malnutrition and hunger are the number one risks to health worldwide. An increasing population is not the only reason we'll need more food, though. As developing nations become more prosperous, they demand more meat, eggs, and dairy—which means growing more soybeans and corn to feed the animals that provide these foods.

Problems of hunger are far more complex than just producing enough food, however. Places where people suffer the most from hunger are typically places where there is war or other civil strife, political instability, extreme weather events, or natural disasters. In 2016, the United Nations estimated that 400,000 people in Syria were trapped without access to food and other necessary supplies (such as medicines) in besieged cities due to the civil war there. Two of the countries with the most alarming levels of hunger over the past few years, Central African Republic and Chad, have both experienced political instability for several years. A month after Hurricane Matthew devastated Haiti in 2016, the *Washington Post* reported that 800,000 people there were in urgent need of food. Other disasters, such as the earthquakes, floods, and droughts, have similar results.

Even if we could end war and prevent natural disasters, we would still need more food. Most experts agree that in the coming years, if there is to be enough food for the world's population, we have to give some serious thought to increasing food production, as well as to addressing issues of how to get that food into hungry mouths.

The question about the best way to do this has become increasingly pressing, yet the arguments are often polarized, with some arguing the only way to produce enough food is to increase yields with the latest in farming technology and centralized production by industrial corporate farming. Others argue just as passionately that such techniques are not only unnecessary, they are the wrong way to go about the problem; that in fact the only way to feed an increasing world population is by decentralizing agriculture and putting ownership of farms in the hands of small, local farmers.

In this chapter you will read arguments on both sides of the debate—and some that see the problem as more nuanced and complex than is often obvious from the headlines.

> "The demonization of 'industrial farming' serves no constructive purpose. Yes, modern farming is 'industrial.' It has to be."

Industrial Farming May Not Be as Bad as We Think

Steve Savage

In the following viewpoint, Steve Savage draws on United States Department of Agriculture (USDA) data, as well as his own experience working on industrial farms in addition to family farms, to argue that industrial farming is necessary to feed the world. Though he also argues that many of the criticisms of industrial farming are overblown, he offers some suggestions for improving the environmental effects of industrial farming. Savage has a PhD in plant pathology and over the past thirty years has worked for both universities and corporations, including DuPont, Mycogen, and Colorado State University.

"You Talk About 'Industrial Farming' Like It's A Bad Thing!" by Steve Savage, Sustainable Enterprises Media, Inc., February 4, 2010. Reprinted by permission.

As you read, consider the following questions:

1. Does Savage's description of life on a "family owned" industrial farm change your image of large-scale farming?

2. How does Savage say agriculture has changed since the 1930s?

3. Do the author's suggestions for "Agriculture 2.0" seem feasible in light of what he says elsewhere in the article?

The phrase, "industrial farming" is something I see on lots of web posts and comment strings. I'm guessing that this intentionally derisive terminology conjures up some pretty negative imagery for most people not directly involved with farming. The use of this emotive term raises two questions for me:

- Is modern, "industrial" farming actually what people imagine it to be?
- Is there actually a viable alternative?

Well, let's consider some of the features of modern farming:

"Industrial Farming Is Highly Mechanized" (True But Necessary)

It might not fit your view of a romantic, rural life-style, but if you are actually the farmer, the comfortable, efficient, sophisticated farm equipment available today sounds pretty good. As in all "industrialized" segments of our economy, machines and computers make farmers more productive and eliminate the most laborious (and often dangerous) parts of the job. There is a detailed history of farm equipment on the John Deere website that is worth a read. Mechanization of farming has enabled the workforce directly involved in farming to drop from approximately 40 percent in 1900 to less than one percent today. Over this time period, people have chosen other careers intentionally. There are not a lot of people who want to work on farms in the old, labor-intensive way.

Actually, hand-labor-intensive crops (e.g. coffee, strawberries…), or high labor cropping systems (e.g. Organic) are on a collision course with demographic trends. The pool of unskilled farm laborers upon which rich Americans have (unethically) depended is only going to decline over time and make rejection of "mechanization" an increasingly non-viable option. Unless you are the one doing the work, it isn't really reasonable to insist that mechanization be avoided because it's too "industrial."

"Industrial Farming Is Largely Corporate" (False)

The widely held image of US Agriculture as "corporate" turns out to be in direct conflict with the facts. The USDA tracks this in the "Census of Agriculture" that it conducts every 5 years. It isn't completely accurate because it does not differentiate between real "corporations" owned by uninvolved stockholders from farming operations that are conducted by an extended family and just put under a corporate structure for tax/estate-planning reasons. Even so, the vast, vast majority of farming is still on family farms. That is not surprising. Farming is a highly risky and not highly profitable venture. Try selling that on Wall Street! The most "corporate" sectors of farming are in fresh produce where scale is critical to be able to respond to the leverage of the retail industry. Fresh produce is a tiny part of agriculture on an area basis.

"Industrial Farming Is Large-Scale" (True, But Not Probably Like What You Think)

If I told you that I have visited 5,000 to 12,000 acre farms you might imagine something, well, "industrial." I've met with many such growers and my interviews were with the one to two family members to do almost all the farming. We met at the kitchen table or in a corner of the machine shed where there might be a sticky, runt calf under heating lights being bottle fed. Even these seemingly huge operations are family farms. Because of the mechanization I've described, an extremely large grain farm can be run by a very small number of people who often work off-farm as well. Still, if you met these farmers, they would perfectly fit your image of "the salt of the earth, hard-working folks," and you would also see that they are quite concerned with the environment. In fact, large farms have a higher adoption rate of the most sustainable practices I will describe below.

Actually, there is a trend both towards large farms and small farms. Between 2002 and 2007 there was a small increase in large farms, but a huge increase in the number of very small farms. There are a lot of complex and region-specific dynamics here, but just the fact that much of farm acreage is in larger farms does not need to be a big concern. If you don't believe me, go meet some of the folks that run the large farms.

"Industrial Farms Use Synthetic Fertilizer, Hybrid Seeds and Pesticides" (True, But the Alternatives Are Not So Great)

Historical Crop Yield Progress in the United States

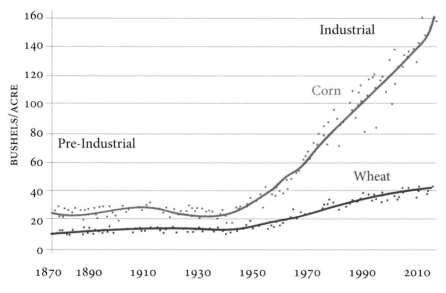

SOURCE: USDA NASS

The graph above shows that "Pre-industrial" yields were low and stagnant over 60 years. The amazing yield gains in the "industrial era" came first from synthetic fertilizers, then from improved plant breeding, pesticides, and most recently biotechnology.

Along the way there were definitely environmental issues with the way farming was being done, but also changes and improvements. The Dust Bowl calamity of the 1930s lead to the establishment of the Soil Conservation Service as the first step towards improving farming practices. The pioneers of "no-till" agriculture got started in the early 60s working to save fuel and stop erosion. The Environmental Movement of the late 60s lead to the establishment of the EPA in 1969, and pesticides have changed dramatically. By the time I started working in agriculture in 1977 there was already a major research effort focused on improving the environmental and safety profile of agriculture. Since that time I've had the privilege of working with a wide range of public and private scientists and with farmers to see these improvements implemented.

An Ideal for Industrial Agriculture

Even though mainstream industrial agriculture has come a long way, there is an even better "suite" of sustainable practices that would ideally see further adoption. I sometimes call these the elements of "Agriculture 2.0."

- Continuous "No-till" (saves fuel, stores moisture better, eliminates erosion and off-site movement of pollutants, increases biodiversity)
- Cover-Cropping (with no-till leads to net carbon sequestration, can be used either to produce biologically fixed nitrogen or to scavenge excess nitrate as needed)
- Controlled Wheel Traffic (saves fuel, stops compaction, reduces nitrous oxide emissions)
- Precision, Variable-Rate Fertilization (reduces fertilizer need, and nitrous oxide)

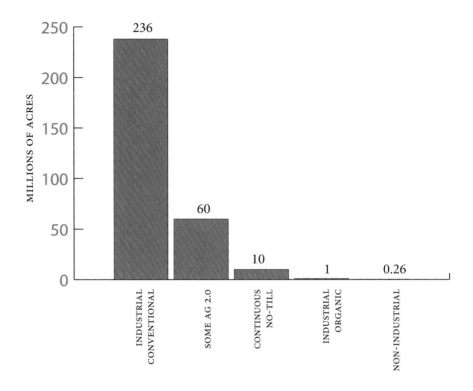

US Harvested Cropland Acreage in 2007

Considering Scale

There were 309.5 million acres of harvested cropland in the US according to the 2007 Census of Agriculture. Even after 30 years of "rapid growth," only 1.29 million of those were Organic. But an anti-industrial purist would only consider a small part of that (at most 20%) to be truly non-industrial. What about "Ag 2.0"? Unfortunately, the Bush administration cut funding to the CTIC (the organization that used to track things like tillage practices). Groups like CTIC now estimate that, 5-10% of the corn/soy rotation (~10 million acres) in the US are farmed with "continuous no-till" —the most important feature of Ag 2.0. I estimate that the total area that is utilizing at least some Ag 2.0 practices is on the order of 70 million acres or possibly higher. Looking at this graph, which sustainable alternative looks to have the most realistic potential for growth?

Non-Industrial Farms Exist (True, But the model Is Not Scalable)

I'm all for small-scale, local farms, CSAs, gardens, and the like, it is just that this cannot be extrapolated as the kind of farming that will feed the US population, let alone the millions of people around the world who depend on US agriculture. To think that it can is actually a dangerous delusion that is wide-spread among our non-farming population. People just don't understand the scale of food production that is needed.

The demonization of "industrial farming" serves no constructive purpose. Yes, modern farming is "industrial." It has to be. Like any industry, farming can be improved from an environmental point of view (and it has, dramatically). We will accomplish a lot more for the environment and for humanity by supporting the further adoption of "Agriculture 2.0" practices on "industrial" farms than by pretending we don't need it.

> *"The question then, is not 'how to feed the world,' but rather, how can we develop sustainable farming methods that have the potential to help the world feed and sustain itself."*

Corporate, Industrial Agriculture Has Already Failed to Feed the World

Dawn Gifford

In the following viewpoint, Dawn Gifford explains why industrial agriculture has failed to feed the world and offers specific suggestions for how agriculture can do a better job. She specifically challenges much of the reasoning supporting the argument that high-tech agriculture is necessary to feed the world and gives examples of programs and policies that have reduced hunger. In addition, she draws a clear distinction between merely feeding people and providing good nutrition. Gifford maintains the website Small Footprint Family. She is a master gardener, master composter, and a former horticulture teacher and extension agent.

As you read, consider the following questions:
1. Why is starvation and child malnourishment high in India, even though they have global exports of food?
2. How did Belo Horizonte, Brazil, end hunger in that city?
3. What does the author claim is the difference between feeding people and solving their nutrition problems?

There are a lot of myths about our ability to "feed the world." Many people think that without high-tech inputs like genetically engineered crops (GMOs), pesticides, and synthetic fertilizers, we will have widespread famine as the global population mushrooms to 8 or 9 billion people over the coming decades.

Nothing could be further from the truth...

The Number One Myth About Hunger

The number one myth about hunger is that we simply don't produce enough food to feel the billions of people who will be on the planet by 2050.

This is a lie.

According to the United Nations Food & Agriculture Organization (UNFAO) 2007 report,

> Current food production can sustain world food needs even for the 8 billion people projected to inhabit the planet by 2030. This will hold even with anticipated increases in meat consumption, and without adding genetically modified crops.

And given that Western countries *waste* about 40% of all their food, yet still have hungry people, producing enough is not really the issue. Think about it: Hunger is not primarily because of a lack of food, but rather because the hungry are too poor to buy the food that is available.

Nobel laureate Amartya Sen is most famous for proving that famine is fundamentally a problem of *democracy, poverty, and food distribution.* The globe's farms are already producing enough food to feed 12 billion people—twice the current population and a third more than the peak of 9 billion expected to be reached in 2050.

Yet at least a billion people lack access to enough to eat. For example, nearly half of the African continent's 750 million people subsist on less than one dollar a day—nearly twice as many as 25 years ago. They are too poor to buy the food that is available but often poorly distributed, or they lack the land and resources to grow it themselves.

Raising crop yields does not prevent hunger or famine. Over the last 30 years, the Indian sub-continent went from being a chronic food importer to a massive grain exporter, but this did not keep 200 million Indians from going hungry in 1995 while the country exported $625 million worth of wheat and flour and 5 million metric tons of rice.

Starvation deaths and child malnutrition are common in India, despite the fact that India ranks near the top of agricultural exporters in the global south. India's current 26 million-ton grain surplus could easily feed its 320 million hungry people, but it does not. Why? Because starving villagers are too poor to buy the food produced in their own countryside.

You can see this to a lesser extent in the U.S., where *16.7 million children* (that's 1 in 5 children!) don't have enough to eat because their parents cannot afford to buy all the food they need. Meanwhile, a mean-spirited segment of our society wants to eliminate Food Stamps and school lunch programs, both of which barely provide adequate nutrition to growing young bodies, but are all we currently have to help ensure the general welfare of poor children.

Ending Hunger Is Cheap and Easy

In stark contrast to the U.S., the city of Belo Horizonte, Brazil has effectively *ended hunger* in their city once and for all. Belo, a city of 2.5 million people, once had 11 percent of its population living in absolute poverty, and almost 20 percent of its children going hungry.

Then in 1993, a newly elected administration *declared food a right of citizenship*. The new mayor said, in effect: If you are too poor to buy food in the market—you are no less a citizen. I am still accountable to you.

During the first six years of Belo's food-as-a-right policy, the city agency developed dozens of innovations to assure everyone the right to food, especially by weaving together the interests of farmers and consumers.

It offered local family farmers dozens of choice spots of public space on which to sell to urban consumers, essentially redistributing retailer mark-ups on produce—which often reached 100 percent—to consumers and the farmers. Farmers' profits grew, since there was no wholesaler taking a cut. And poor people got access to fresh, healthy, local food.

In addition to the farmer-run stands, the city makes healthy food available by offering entrepreneurs the opportunity to bid on the right to use well-trafficked plots of city land for local supermarkets. Today there are 34 such markets where the city determines a set price—about two-thirds of the market price—of about twenty healthy items. Everything else they can sell at the market price.

Belo's food security initiatives also include reduced-price community cafés offering fresh, local food, extensive community and school gardens, and nutrition classes. Plus, money the federal government contributes toward school lunches, once spent on processed, corporate food, now buys whole food, mostly from local growers.

In just a decade Belo Horizonte cut its infant death rate—widely used as evidence of hunger—by more than half, and today these initiatives benefit almost 40 percent of the city's 2.5 million population to varying degrees. One six-month period in 1999 saw infant malnutrition in a sample group reduced by 50 percent. And between 1993 and 2002 Belo Horizonte was the only locality in Brazil in which consumption of fruits and vegetables went up.

The cost of these efforts?

Around $10 million annually, or *less than 2 percent of the city budget.* That's about a penny a day per Belo resident.

When asked if she realized how important what she was doing was, how rare in the world it is was to treat food as a right of citizenship, a Belo city manager replied tearfully,

> I knew we had so much hunger in the world, but what is so upsetting, what I didn't know when I started this, is it's so easy. It's so easy to end it.

Why Crop Yield *Doesn't* Matter—A Brief History of Today's Agriculture

Launched in the 1960s, the Green Revolution aimed to increase grain yields through the use of new agricultural technologies. The Green Revolution promoted the use of hybrid seed varieties that could be densely planted and required irrigation, mechanization, and the heavy application of chemical fertilizers and pesticides to get higher yields.

The underlying objective of the Green Revolution was to increase farm productivity in countries perceived to be susceptible to communism because of rural poverty and hunger. But rather than raising production by redressing highly unequal land ownership, however, the Green Revolution favored technological fixes.

By the 1970s, it became apparent that by not addressing underlying social, political and economic injustices, the Green Revolution technologies only favored rich farmers and accentuated social inequalities. As a result, millions of smallholder farmers were forced out of agriculture, and migrated to the city, forming the massive, infamous slums now common throughout India, Latin America, and other parts of the developing world. Others began farming fragile hillsides and marginal lands, leading to persistent poverty and deforestation.

As a result, between 1970 and 1990, while the total available food in the developing world rose by 11 percent, the number of hungry people also rose by 11 percent. In Latin America, the number of hungry people rose by 18 percent. (China was the exception. Unlike India and Latin America, it brought down the number of hungry people through a combination of modernization and massive land reforms.)

By the 1990s an estimated 95 percent of all farmers in the First World and 40 percent of all farmers in the Third World were using Green Revolution hybrid seeds, with the greatest use found in Asia, followed by Mexico and Latin America. The world lost an estimated 75 percent of its food biodiversity, and control over seeds shifted from farming communities to a handful of multinational corporations.

In the long run, the Green Revolution has proved to be *anything but* green. Farming methods that depend heavily on machinery and agrochemicals erode the soil's natural fertility over time. As fertility decreases and pests build tolerance, farmers have to apply more and more fertilizer and pesticides to get the same results.

In Punjab, India, an early Green Revolution showcase, farmers now apply three times the amount of fertilizers to maintain the same yields. They are also running out of groundwater and losing increasingly larger portions of their crops to pesticide-resistant insects and weeds.

Similar trends can be seen in the U.S., too, especially in the midwest where most of the industrial grain and soy monocultures are grown. Soil infertility, superweeds and superbugs threaten American farms unlike ever before, and today, farmers are resorting to ever more toxic measures to combat them, including using chemicals known to cause cancer and birth defects, like Dicamba and 2-4-D, which is basically *Agent Orange* [a powerful defoliant used by the US military in the Vietnam War].

Today's Farming Methods Cannot Be Sustained

The evidence against the Green Revolution is overwhelming: The industrial practices and synthetic chemicals introduced to the world during the 60s have *ravaged* the environment, caused dramatic loss of biodiversity and associated traditional knowledge, favored wealthier farmers and multinational agribusiness, and left many poor farmers deep in debt, and displaced from the land.

Today, there is a *new* Green Revolution proposed for Africa by the Alliance for a Green Revolution in Africa (AGRA), an organization funded by the Bill and Melinda Gates Foundation, which supports Monsanto and GMO crops. Unfortunately, this new revolution appears destined to repeat the tragic record left by the first one, by increasing dependency on foreign aid, fossil fuels, foreign inputs and patent-protected GM seed varieties which poor farmers cannot afford.

But, the growing push toward industrial agriculture and globalization of the food system—with an emphasis on export crops, genetically modified crops, and rapid expansion of biofuel crops (sugar cane, corn, soybean, oil palm, eucalyptus, etc.)—is increasingly reshaping the world's agriculture and food supply, with potentially severe economic, social, and ecological impacts and risks. After all, *none of these commodity crops actually feed people the diverse, nutritious diet that we need to be healthy.*

Furthermore, the industrial farming practices currently in use today (including industrial-scale organic farming to a lesser degree) release *tons* of harmful carbon dioxide and nitrogen into the atmosphere; deplete precious phosphorus and potash reserves; and promote soil erosion, salinization, desertification and loss of soil fertility. In fact, from clearing a field to delivery to your table, *nothing* releases more carbon dioxide, nitrous oxide and methane into the atmosphere than industrial agriculture.

The UNFAO estimates that over 25 percent of arable land in the world is already compromised by these problems, especially in more arid regions and in sloped terrain. And with recent droughts induced by climate change, the U.S. (and other countries) could be facing another catastrophic Dust Bowl in the coming decade, if we don't change the way we farm, and *fast.*

Why would we want to export such destruction to developing countries, knowing it will immediately come back around to harm us all?

So, How Do We "Feed the World"?

"Feeding the world" is industrial agriculture's claim to the moral high ground and with that claim, they justify the chemicals, fossil fuels and all the pollution, resource depletion, and soil destruction.

But did you know that U.S. farmers do not, actually "feed the world"? At least not directly, anyway.

Margaret Mellon, a scientist with the environmental advocacy group Union of Concerned Scientists, recently wrote an essay in which she claims it's time to set the idea of "feeding the world" aside. It doesn't answer the concerns about sustainability and the environment that people have about modern agriculture—and it's not even true.

"Industrial farming in America doesn't really grow food for hungry people," she says in a recent NPR piece. Forty percent of the biggest crop in the U.S.—corn—goes into ethanol fuel for cars. And much of the rest of our corn crop goes into livestock feed and food additives like corn syrup that provide little nutritional value. Most of the second-biggest crop—soybeans—is fed to animals. What is left is sold on the commodity market.

Growing more grain isn't the solution to hunger anyway, Mellon says. If you're really trying to solve that problem, there are many other things we can do that are much more important: "We need to empower women; we need to raise incomes; we need infrastructure in the developing world; we need the ability to get food to market without spoiling."

Indirectly, bigger harvests in the U.S. do tend to make food more affordable around the world simply by driving the cost down. And since hunger is a *poverty* issue, not a productivity issue, lower food prices are a good thing for poor people. For instance, Chinese pigs are growing fat on cheap soybean meal grown by farmers in the United States and Brazil, and that's one reason why hundreds of millions of people in China are eating much better than a generation ago—they can afford to buy pork.

This is a good thing in the short term, however it comes at a grave environmental and social cost in the long run. Driving prices down means that everyone gets paid less, including the small family corn farmer in Africa who just can't compete with cheap U.S. exports.

And if that weren't trouble enough, the big crops that American farmers send abroad simply don't provide the vitamins and minerals that billions of people need most. So if the U.S. exports lots of corn, driving down the cost of cornmeal, it drives poor families to buy lots of cornmeal, and to buy less in the way of leafy green vegetables, or milk or eggs, that have the key nutrients that provide good health.

In this case, the U.S. is *kind of* feeding people, but definitely *not* solving their nutrition problems.

But there is a fundamental flaw in the whole "feeding the world" concept in the first place:

North Dakota organic farmer and distinguished fellow at the Leopold Center for Sustainable Agriculture, Fred Kirschenmann refutes the notion that industrial, high-input production for the global marketplace is the only way to feed the world. Kirschenmann even wonders if "feeding the world" should be our goal.

> "Feeding the world" suggests that someone will take responsibility for feeding someone else, and therefore make them dependent. Under those terms, there can be no food security. "Keeping the world fed" suggests that people will be empowered to feed themselves. That is essential to long-term food security.

Critics of sustainable, organic farming often argue that such methods can't keep up the pace of producing enough food to feed an ever-expanding human population. But Kirschenmann maintains that we need alternatives to the industrial model because it is quickly destroying the fragile ecological balances and using up the natural resources upon which farming depends. And people still aren't getting fed. "The real problem with the unprecedented increase in human population is that it has led to the disruption and deterioration of the natural functioning of earth's biotic community, and *that is what threatens our future—not lack of production*," he points out.

THERE IS NO ONE SOLUTION TO FEEDING THE HUNGRY

In December of 2007, Dr. Jacques Diouf, Director-General of the Food and Agriculture Organisation (FAO) of the United Nations, commented on a press report suggesting that FAO endorses organic agriculture (OA) as the solution to world hunger. "We should use organic agriculture and promote it," Dr. Diouf said. "It produces wholesome, nutritious food and represents a growing source of income for developed and developing countries. But you cannot feed six billion people today and nine billion in 2050 without judicious use of chemical fertilizers."

[...]

Judicious use of chemical inputs, especially fertilizers, could help significantly boost food production in Sub-Saharan Africa, where farmers use less than one tenth of the fertilizer applied by their Asian counterparts, Dr. Diouf said…. In its annual World Development Report, the World Bank noted this year, that "low fertilizer use is one of the major constraints on increasing agricultural productivity in Sub-Sahara Africa." "However, chemical inputs must be used with care," Dr. Diouf said. … Higher productivity with lower inputs can be obtained from such systems as Integrated Pest Management (IPM) and Conservation Agriculture (CA), Dr. Diouf noted. IPM can reduce pesticide use by 50% in the case of cotton and vegetable production and up to 100 percent with rice. CA and no-tillage agriculture reduces labour requirements by doing away with ploughing and can use 30 percent less fertilizer and 20 percent less pesticides.

The key elements in feeding the world now and in the future will be increased public and private investments, the right policies and technologies, knowledge and capacity building, grounded in sound ecosystem management. "There is no one solution to the problem of feeding the world's hungry and poor," Dr. Diouf concluded.

"Organic Agriculture Can Contribute to Fighting Hunger, But Chemical Fertilizers Needed to Feed the World," by Christopher Matthews, Food and Agriculture Organization of the United Nations (FAO), December 10, 2007.

Reducing waste, slowing population growth, and changing our paradigm about the right to food are part of the solution. But the other major piece of the puzzle is to find ways of farming that mirror the evolutionary stability of the ecosystems in which we live, and that enhance and augment, rather than deplete, our natural resources.

After examining ag-related controversies ranging from global climate change to the role of livestock, Kirschenmann argues that organic farms "…integrated into local ecologies and rooted in local communities, can do a better job of *keeping the world fed* than large, corporate farms owned by distant investors."

He concludes: "The best way to achieve food security is through food locally produced by local people with local control."

The Case for Agroecological and Organic Farming

Can organic, smallholder farming feed an increasingly hungry world? Almost everyone assumes that it can't. Organic farming is seen as something purely for the health-conscious Western middle classes. But the truth is counter-intuitive.

Study after study after study shows that organic and agroecological techniques can provide much more food per acre in developing countries than conventional chemical-based agriculture. One report—published 2008 by the United Nations Environment Programme (UNEP) and the UN Conference on Trade and Development (UNCTAD)—found that 114 projects, covering nearly two million African farmers, more than doubled their yields by introducing organic or near-organic practices. And today, some smallholders are breaking all records for productivity!

Numerous field trials in the U.S. and the U.K have shown that organic farming practices produce yields equal to or greater than conventional for fruit and vegetables, but somewhat reduced yields for commodities like wheat and corn, except during drought, when organic outperforms there too.

But even if organic commodity yields are 10-20 percent reduced compared to commodity crops farmed with fossil-fuel dependent machines and toxic chemicals, biodiversity loss, environmental degradation, and severe impacts on ecosystem services have not only accompanied conventional farming systems but have often extended well beyond their field boundaries.

With organic agriculture, environmental costs tend to be lower and the benefits greater.

Overall, organic farms tend to store more soil carbon, have better soil quality, and reduce soil erosion compared to their conventional counterparts. Organic agriculture also creates far less soil and water pollution and lower greenhouse gas emissions. And it's more energy-efficient because it doesn't rely on synthetic fertilizers or pesticides.

Organic agriculture is also associated with greater biodiversity of plants, animals, insects and microbes as well as genetic diversity, which creates a more resilient food system. In severe drought conditions (which are expected to increase with climate change) organic farms often produce higher yields than conventional agriculture because of the higher water-holding capacity of organically farmed soils.

Crop yield simply cannot be the only criteria for a healthy, sustainable agriculture anymore. In fact, a recent report from the U.N. Commission on Trade and Development stated that the only way we are going to maintain global security and stop escalating conflicts is through meeting the "urgent need to transform agriculture toward a rapid and significant shift from conventional, monoculture-based and high-external-input-dependent industrial production toward mosaics of sustainable, regenerative production systems that also considerably improve the productivity of small-scale farmers."

Agroecological, organic techniques like polycultural plantings, guild stacking, rotation crops, cover crops and animal manures are particularly advantageous in regions that lack money, technology and fossil fuels for industrial approaches. Going organic will also pay long-term dividends, for it *builds up* soil, whereas mechanized, chemical farming depletes it.

Organic also prevents exposure to toxic pesticides, increases local biodiversity, sequesters tons of carbon which offsets global warming, and stores more water in the ground in what will be an increasingly hot, thirsty world.

Professor Jules Pretty of Essex University, who has studied the issue for more than 20 years, says: "Methods used by organic farmers can dramatically increase yields over those achieved by low-intensity conventional agriculture." Even more important, as the UN's International Fund for Agricultural Development points out, going organic almost always boosts the incomes of small Third World farmers, because they no longer have to buy costly inputs.

Poor farmers around the world are lifting themselves out of poverty by going organic. Small-scale farmers *all over the world* have stopped forking out for expensive, toxic chemicals and patented, genetically modified seeds in favor of traditional methods of growing which they haven't used for decades.

The result? Small communities are re-learning how to manage their natural resources, meaning they produce more reliable, bigger crops and a better living wage with less toxic pollution. For many of the world's 1.4 billion small-scale farmers, the benefit of using agroecological farming methods is clear: better food, more security and a better life.

A New Way for the Post-Fossil Fuel World

"The commercial industrial technologies that are used in agriculture today to feed the world… are not inherently sustainable," former Monsanto CEO Robert Shapiro told the Society of Environmental Journalists in 1995. "They have not worked well to promote either self-sufficiency or food security in developing countries." Feeding the world sustainably "is out of the question with current agricultural practice," says Shapiro. "Loss of topsoil, of salinity of soil as a result of irrigation, and ultimate reliance on petrochemicals … are, obviously, not renewable. That clearly isn't sustainable."

Wow! Can you believe these words came out of the mouth of a Monsanto CEO? Well, while he may be right about the problem, do we really need to embark upon another risky technological, industrial fix (like GMOs) to solve the mistakes of a previous one?

Instead, we should be looking for solutions that are based on ecological and biological principles and have few, if any, environmental and social costs. Fortunately, there is such an alternative that has been pioneered by organic farmers and permaculture smallholders worldwide.

In contrast to the industrial monoculture approach advocated by Monsanto and the GM seed industry, organic agriculture is described by the United Nations Food & Agriculture Organization (FAO) as "a holistic production management system which promotes and enhances agro-ecosystem health, including biodiversity, biological cycles, and soil biological activity."

According to Miguel A. Altieri, professor of agroecology at the University of California at Berkeley, "Food systems must become less dependent on fossil fuels, more resilient in the face of climate change, and able to contribute to the Government's pledge to cut greenhouse gas emissions by 80 percent by 2050. Farming based on organic principles can deliver against all three challenges."

In 2008, the world's biggest and most authoritative study— the International Assessment of Agricultural Knowledge, Science and Technology for Development (IAASTD)—advocated organic agriculture as part of a "radical change" in the way the world grows its food. Certainly, the present over-concentration on intensive agriculture has not succeeded even in reducing the number of people going hungry—in 2009, it topped one billion for the first time.

Technology will of course be important to the looming food crisis, but the search for a "silver bullet" like genetic modification to solve all these problems is a dangerous distraction. The solutions are already largely available all around us; it's now about the political will to implement them.

The question then, is not "how to feed the world," but rather, how can we develop sustainable farming methods that have the potential to help the world *feed and sustain itself.*

7 Steps to "Keeping the World Fed"

According to *Yes!* Magazine, "The official prescriptions for solving the world food crisis call for more subsidies for industrialized nations, more food aid, and more so-called Green (or Gene) Revolutions. Expecting the institutions that built the current flawed food system to solve the food crisis is like asking an arsonist to put out a forest fire.

When the world food crisis exploded in early 2008, ADM's profits increased by 38 percent, Cargill's by 128 percent, and Mosaic Fertilizer (a Cargill subsidiary) by a whopping 1,615 percent! Meanwhile, millions starved all over the world.

For decades, family farmers the world over have resisted this corporate control. They have worked to diversify crops, protect soil and native seeds, and conserve nature. They have established local gardens, businesses, and community-based food systems. These strategies are effective. They need to be given a chance to work.

The solutions to the food crisis are those that make the lives of family farmers easier: re-regulate the market, reduce the power of the agri-foods industrial complex, and build ecologically resilient family and community agriculture.

Here are some of the recommended steps:

1. Support domestic food production.
2. Stabilize and guarantee fair prices to farmers and consumers by re-establishing floor prices and publicly owned national grain reserves. Establish living wages for workers on farms, in processing facilities, and in supermarkets.
3. Halt agrofuels expansion.
4. Curb speculation in food.
5. Promote a return to smallholder farming. On a pound-per-acre basis, family farms are substantially more productive than large-scale industrial farms. And they use less oil, less water and fewer chemicals. Because

75 percent of the world's poor are farmers, this will
address poverty, too.

6. Support agro-ecological and organic food production.
7. Food sovereignty: Recognize the right of all people to
healthy and culturally appropriate food produced through
ecologically sound methods and their own food systems."

Can Organic Farming Feed the World?

So, can organic farming feed the world? ...Or, rather, *keep the
world fed*?

I would argue it is the only thing that can.

> "Some 850 million people don't have enough to eat. Perversely some 1.4 billion people are overweight, 600 million of them obese. Both groups suffer from micronutrient malnutrition, a lack of key vitamins and minerals."

Sustainable Farming Methods Will Provide Not Just More Food, but Better Food

Zareen Pervez Bharucha

In the following viewpoint, Zareen Pervez Bharucha argues that the current agricultural system has failed to meet the nutritional needs of the world population. While millions go hungry, almost as many are obese, suffering a different kind of malnutrition. The answer, she says, is not simply increasing yields but growing more nutritious food in a more sustainable way. In addition, she addresses the social, political, and structural issues of how to make sure that food actually reaches the people who need it. Bharucha is senior research officer at the Department of Sociology, University of Sussex. She recently completed post-doctoral research on the links between local food and psychological well-being in the East of England.

"How to Feed Nine Billion People, and Feed Them Well," by Zareen Pervez Bharucha, The Conversation, January 8, 2014. https://theconversation.com/how-to-feed-nine-billion-people-and-feed-them-well-19876. Licensed Under CC BY-ND 4.0 International.

As you read, consider the following questions:

1. How does the author say global agriculture has failed?
2. Why does she say that simply increasing yields of the same crops will not help reduce hunger?
3. Why does the author say that grain surpluses in India often never reach the hungry?

Resource-intensive agriculture, despite its productivity, nevertheless has failed to feed the world's current population, never mind the nine billion people expected by 2050. This system that currently fails both people and planet is ripe for revision.

We need to be more ambitious, to go beyond simply producing more. We need to produce more of what's good—not just cereal staples, but nutrition-dense foods—in ways that can prevent or even reverse land degradation, encourage biodiversity, conserve water, and allow the world's poor more equal access to land, food, and markets than has historically been the case.

There is a significant "triple burden" of malnutrition. Some 850 million people don't have enough to eat. Perversely some 1.4 billion people are overweight, 600 million of them obese. Both groups suffer from micronutrient malnutrition, a lack of key vitamins and minerals. These imbalances mean we ought to examine what exactly is being produced, and how it is distributed. The co-existence of highly productive agricultural systems and hunger, of obesity and starvation, powerfully highlight how global agriculture has failed to substantially narrow economic inequalities, and has perpetuated nutritional imbalances on billions.

And despite its failures, agriculture's costs are high. Crop and livestock production is responsible for half the methane and two-thirds of the nitrous oxide released by humans. The use of nitrous fertiliser has disrupted global nitrogen and phosphorus cycles. And agriculture is a leading driver of global biodiversity loss, something that greatly affects communities around the world that rely on wild species for food and income.

More, but more of what?

We can't simply hope to produce more of the same and feed the world. There are alternative models, but they need recognition and support. However the emphasis on production efficiency is dominant, even in discussions of sustainable agricultural intensification. Here, thought is only given to how to increase supply of cereals and animal products in ever more efficient ways.

The Green Revolution in Latin America and South Asia, for example, resulted in tremendous increases in crop yield. But this was only because new technologies were supported by government subsidies, cheap credit, supportive markets and plentiful irrigation. This increased productivity did not, by itself, result in a better-fed population. It provided an abundance of calorie-rich staple crops such as rice and wheat, but saw the supply of nutrient-rich crops such as pulses and vegetables fall and their cost rise. And this model of intensive irrigation and fertiliser use wasn't an option everywhere. India's Green Revolution was concentrated in the favourable lands of the Punjab, ignoring the rain-fed drylands that support most of the country's farmers.

Even when grown in larger amounts, crops must be accessible and affordable if they are to alleviate hunger. This cannot be left to global markets, whose volatility in recent years has made it substantially harder to alleviate poverty and hunger—a fact recognised by the UN Food and Agriculture Organisation, which has stated "unless local agriculture is developed and/or other income-earning opportunities open up, the food insecurity determined by limited local production will persist, even in the middle of potential plenty at the world level."

So production is necessary, but insufficient: ensuring produce is properly distributed to fair markets is vital. In India for example, it has long been the case due to a lack of proper storage facilities, corruption and inequity in the means of distribution, grain surpluses are simply left to rot without ever reaching the hungry.

Seeing past the status quo

A recent report on food by Robert Craig, highlights just how dominant this "productivist" approach is. The report examines the status of agriculture in Brazil, Chile, Peru, the US, India, China and New Zealand. Craig shows how—while each country presents very different social-ecological conditions—the dominant rhetoric is the same in each: production, profits, demand, supply and prices of major commodities, traded on world markets. Seen through this lens, there is no room for a nuanced ecological approach, let alone awareness of the political, social and economic factors that influence hunger.

Estimates of land and water are pitted against demand projections. "Sustainability" only means using resources efficiently. Complex environments are reduced to either source or sink. The author is told in Peru "if river water reaches the sea it's seen as a waste." He is shown how resources could be developed to meet projected demand: the schemes range from trying to control how much farmers can irrigate in India, to spending £62 billion to bring alive Mao's vision of a canal to transport water from China's southern region to its arid north. This is a scheme that has displaced over 300,000 people, disrupted the southern river basins, and may fail anyway, if climate change leaves them with less water in the southern rivers to draw from.

So are there alternatives? Very much so. There is an emerging global movement that emphasises increased consumer participation in (ostensibly) ecologically sound and socially just food systems. And for increasing production using ecologically sound methods,—so-called sustainable intensification,—there is a great deal of agroecological practice worldwide that is recognised by researchers.

In India, farmers are revitalising rice production by applying principles of the System of Rice Intensification. In some states, the technique has been officially endorsed and supported.

Across Africa, sustainable production practices, designed with farmer participation, have raised yields, and enhanced the agricultural landscape. Such practices have also contributed to a range of human development goals, such as food security, alleviating poverty, and improving skills and knowledge. These systems and practices are designed to do more than just conserve resources and boost yields. More ambitious, they aim to feed people balanced, nutrient-rich diets, while reversing the substantially damaging effects on land, plant and wildlife biodiversity that industrial agriculture has wrought.

> *"Organic production, for all its ecological benefits, is in no position to confront the world's impending demand for food."*

Organic Crops Alone Can't Feed the World

James E. McWilliams

In the following viewpoint, James E. McWilliams builds his argument by citing a study that found crop yields of organic farms were not great enough to feed the world's burgeoning population. The research cited in this article was done by Steve Savage, the author of a previous viewpoint in this chapter. McWilliams believes that organic methods are preferable, but he does not think they are ready to meet the challenge of feeding the world. He agrees with Savage that more investment in agricultural research is needed if we are to develop an agricultural system that is environmentally responsible and sufficient to meet the needs of a growing population. McWilliams is a professor at Texas State University and the author of Just Food: Where Locavores Get It Wrong and How We Can Truly Eat Responsibly.

As you read, consider the following questions:

1. How might rejecting the Western diet make it easier to feed the world using organic methods?

2. What limitations of Savage's study does McWilliams point out?

3. Why does McWillliams say that the lower yields of basic row crops is such a problem when it comes to feeding the world?

The Food and Agriculture Organization predicts that the global population will increase by 2.3 billion between now and 2050. This demographic explosion, intensified by an emerging middle class in China and India, will require the world's farmers to grow at least 70 percent more food than we now produce. Making matters worse, there's precious little arable land left for agricultural expansion. Barring a radical rejection of the Western diet, skyrocketing demand for food will have to be met by increasing production on pre-existing acreage. No matter how effectively we streamline access to existing food supplies, 90 percent of the additional calories required by midcentury will have to come through higher yields per acre.

How this will happen is one of the more contentious issues in agriculture. A particularly vocal group insists that we can avoid a 21st-century Malthusian crisis by transitioning wholesale to organic production—growing food without synthetic chemicals in accordance with the environmentally beneficial principles of agro-ecology. As recently as last September the Rodale Institute, an organization dedicated to the promotion of organic farming, reiterated this precept in no uncertain terms. "Organic farming," it declared, "is the only way to feed the world."

This is an exciting claim. Organic agriculture, after all, is the only approach to growing food that places primary emphasis on enhancing soil health. But is the assertion accurate? Can we actually feed the world with organic agriculture?

New research undertaken by Dr. Steve Savage, an agricultural scientist and plant pathologist, indicates that it's unlikely. In 2008 the USDA's National Agricultural Statistics Service conducted the first comprehensive survey of certified organic agriculture. The study—which had a 90 percent participation rate among U.S. organic farmers who responded to the 2007 Census of Agriculture—recorded acreage, yield, and value for dozens of crops on more than 14,500 farms, in all 50 states.

Savage took these unprecedented USDA/NASS data and compared them with similar USDA statistics from conventional agriculture during the same crop year. (The USDA tallies conventional agriculture stats every year in order to track U.S. agricultural output over time.) The reason why the USDA did not make the comparison to organic production itself is anyone's guess. But what Savage found strongly suggests that organic production, for all its ecological benefits, is in no position to confront the world's impending demand for food.

Perhaps Savage's most striking finding is how few U.S. acres are actually in organic production. Characterizations of organic agriculture routinely portray it as a hard-charging underdog capable of competing for market share with conventional agribusiness. The USDA's Economic Research Service, for example, notes how "Organic agriculture has become one of the fastest growing segments of US agriculture." It's surprising, then, that the 1.6 million acres of harvested organic cropland in 2008 comprised a mere 0.52 percent of total crop acreage in the United States, as Savage found.

Savage's methodology couldn't have been simpler: He lined up and charted organic and conventional yield data for the same crop and state in which they were harvested. Although Savage was working with, as he put it, "the largest such data set on Organic that I have heard of," it wasn't without limitations. The USDA/NASS studies tracked harvested acres without differentiating between irrigated and non-irrigated acreage; it gathered data on planted vs. harvested acres for some crops but not others; it did not account for systems in which "baby vegetable" crops (usually organic) are grown in short rotations on the same plot (such as spinach, lettuce, and carrots) and thus have lower yields; and it omitted some data that would have revealed too much information about individual farmers, in cases where very few growers produce a particular crop.

But even with these qualifications, the numbers are discouraging for the organic option. The rubber really hits the road when it comes to yield. To its credit, organic does quite well in many cases: Sweet potatoes, raspberries, canola, and hay all yielded higher nationally than their conventional counterparts. At the state level, organic squash did better in Oregon than conventional squash; in Arizona and Colorado, organic apples yielded slightly higher than conventional ones; and in Washington state organic peaches beat out conventional varieties. In essence, there's a lot here for organic supporters to cherry-pick as evidence of organic's yield potential (but not cherries, which yielded much lower).

Unfortunately, there's little hope in feeding the world with higher yields of sweet potatoes, peaches, and raspberries—much less hay. What matters most is the performance of basic row-crops. As it turns out, yields were dramatically lower for these commodities: 40 percent lower for winter wheat, 29 percent lower for corn, 34 percent lower for soy, 53 percent lower for spring wheat, 41 percent lower for rice, 58 percent lower for sorghum, and 64 percent lower for millet. Canola was the only row-crop with greater yields with organic farming.

What we might call "secondary staples" did poorly as well. The organic option yielded 28 percent lower for potatoes, 21 percent lower for sweet corn, 38 percent lower for onions, 19 percent lower for snap beans, and 52 percent lower for bell peppers. Perhaps most distressingly, some of the healthiest foods on the planet yielded comparatively poorly under organic production: 42 percent lower for blueberries, 23 percent lower for broccoli, and almost 40 percent lower for tomatoes.

Given these figures, a switch to organic agriculture would require a 43 percent increase over current U.S. cropland, according to Savage. As he puts it, "On a land-area basis, this additional area would be 97% the physical size of Spain or 71% the size of Texas." (Yes, Texas is bigger than Spain.) These are depressing figures, especially in light of the fact that global food demand is entering a 40-year upward trend. It's no wonder that Savage, who spent part of his career developing organic pest controls, concludes that organic "is too small and unproductive to ever be the 'solution' to our need to simultaneously feed the world and protect the environment," as he told me via e-mail.

So should we dismiss organic agriculture outright? Absolutely not. Organic may not be "the" solution to global food demand, but it can certainly be part of it. As Jason Clay, senior vice president of the World Wildlife Fund, writes, "I think we need a new kind of agriculture—kind of a third agriculture, between the big agribusiness, commercial approach to agriculture, and the lessons from organic and local systems." With enhanced investment in agricultural research, there's every reason to hope that organic yields will improve and that the organic model will become more prominent. The fact that we're not yet there, as Savage's study verifies, doesn't mean we should abandon the quest for agricultural systems that are both high yielding and as ecologically responsible as they can be.

> "If we invested in organic agricultural research and development we'd no doubt see a large increase in the yield too."

Organic Farming Methods Are Almost as Productive as Conventional Methods

Lauren C. Ponisio

In the following viewpoint, Lauren C. Ponisio asks if organic farming techniques can produce enough food to feed the world. She analyzes the data and says that organic farming is almost as productive as conventional methods—if done correctly. More research and development could increase the efficiency of organic methods, while simply cutting food waste in half could easily close the gap, she says. Here, she suggests some ways to address the problems brought up in the previous viewpoint. Ponisio is a conservation biologist and a doctoral candidate in conservation biology at the University of California.

As you read, consider the following questions:
1. What is a meta-analysis, and why did Ponisio use it for her analysis?
2. Why do you think Ponisio's results are or are not better than previous studies comparing the two types of farming?
3. What besides increasing yields does Ponisio say needs to be done to address the problems of hunger and obesity.

The unintended consequences of our agricultural food system—polluted air and water, dead zones in coastal seas, soil erosion—have profound implications for human health and the environment. So more sustainable agricultural practices are needed as soon as possible.

Some farmers have turned to less chemically-intensive techniques to reduce the negative impact of agriculture, such as organic farming, which has been shown to outperform conventional farming by many standards of environmental sustainability. The question is whether we can meet these environmental standards and still meet the demand for food, which is predicted to rise substantially in the next 50 years.

Comparing food systems

In our new study, published in Proceedings of the Royal Society B, we found that organic farming systems, when done right, come close to matching the productivity of conventional systems.

Designing a single experiment that could possibly represent the huge variation in crops, weather and soil necessary to get a complete answer is impossible. Instead, we examined the many specific studies that have already been conducted and combined their results—a meta-analysis. We compiled studies from across the globe that compared organic and conventional yields over three decades, representing more than 1,000 comparisons of 52 crop species from 38 countries.

New Technologies Aim to Help Feed the World's Growing Population

Over the next 35 years, an additional two billion humans will be jockeying for a seat at the communal table, requiring an increase in food supply of at least 60%, according to the UN Food and Agriculture Organization. Achieving this growth will require the deployment of technology.

Big Ag is already leveraging big data in the form of "precision farming" and "prescription planting." Large soya and maize farms, for example, are now using a combination of sensors, drones, crop-yield data, satellite images and microclimate forecasting to determine the right number of seeds per acre. Big data solutions also exist to help them optimise water use.

Improving the quality of fertilisers and reducing their environmental impact will be another way to address the food supply challenge. According to the US Environmental Protection Agency, for example, as much as 25% of the nitrogen applied to corn is not absorbed; the runoff makes its way to rivers, groundwater and oceans, causing algae blooms and hypoxia zones where marine life cannot survive.

In an effort to address the problem, a company called California Safe Soil (CSS) converts organic waste from supermarkets into a liquid fertiliser that CSS claims is both cleaner and makes plants more efficient at absorption. Another option, being explored in the pesticide sector by Israeli start-up Catalyst Agtech, is to disintegrate the pollutant before it reaches the groundwater reservoir in the first place. Its patented product, which the company says is compatible with 40% of existing agrochemicals used in the industry, breaks down pesticides' compounds once they reach the deeper, anaerobic layers of the soil—thus limiting the flow of pollutants into groundwater.

"The Technology That Will Help Feed 9 Billion People," by Holly Hickman, World Economic Forum, May 19, 2015.

This isn't the first time researchers have attempted to answer this question, but previous studies have had conflicting results. Combining studies carried out by different scientists for different reasons is a big challenge. Depending on what data is included and how it is handled, answers can vary substantially. Many previous studies found organic yields were 8-25% lower than conventional systems. Another study found that organic farming outperformed conventional in developing countries. In revisiting this question, we used the most extensive dataset to date and methods that try to account for the complexity of the data.

A mirror to nature

We found that although organic crop yields are about 19% lower than conventional yields, certain management practises appear to significantly reduce this gap. In fact, planting multiple different crops at the same time (polyculture) and planting a sequence of crops (crop rotation) on an organic farm cut the difference in yield in half. Interestingly, both these practices are based on techniques that mimic natural systems, and have been practised for thousands of years. Our study strongly suggests that we can develop highly productive organic farming methods if we mimic nature by creating ecologically diverse farms that draw strength from natural interactions between species.

Crop rotation and polycultures are known to improve soil health and reduce pest pressure. Because these practices add diversity to the landscape they also support biodiversity, so they may improve yields while also protecting the environment.

We also found that for some crops such as oats, tomatoes and apples there were no differences in yield between organic and industrial farming at all. The largest yield gaps were found in two cereal crops, wheat and barley. However, since the agricultural Green Revolution in the mid-20th century, improving the yields of cereals grown using conventional, industrial agriculture has received a huge amount of research and funding—far more than organic agriculture. Little wonder, then, that we see a large difference in yields.

For example, some seeds are specifically bred to work well in the nutrient-rich, pest-free conditions found in conventional farms due to the heavy use of fertilisers and pesticides, so they may underperform in organic farms. But if we invested in organic agricultural research and development we'd no doubt see a large increase in the yield too.

We also found evidence that the yield gap estimate we and others have calculated is likely an overestimate. We found evidence of bias in the studies we compiled, which favoured the reporting of higher conventional yields relative to organic. This can arise for several reasons: the studies can favour specific crops or practices so that the results are unrepresentative, or introduce bias during the selection of results to be published. It's impossible to know the origins of the bias, but it's necessary to acknowledge the effect it will have on yield estimates.

Won't solve everything

It's important to remember that simply growing more food is not enough to address the twin crises of hunger and obesity. Current global food production already greatly exceeds what is needed to feed the world's population, yet social, political, and economic factors prevent many people from living well-fed, healthy lives. A focus solely on increased yields will not solve the problem of world hunger.

To put the yield gap into context, the world's food waste alone is 30-40% of food production per year. If food waste were cut by half, this would more than compensate for the difference in yield from converting to organic agriculture, as well as greatly reducing the environmental impact of agriculture.

> *"Some experts think that a more*
> *hopeful, and reasonable, way*
> *forward is a sort of middle ground,*
> *where more and more farmers*
> *adopt the principles of organic*
> *farming even if they don't follow the*
> *approach religiously."*

"Can Organic Farming Feed the World?" Is Not Even the Right Question

Brian Halweil

In the following viewpoint, Brian Halweil builds on viewpoints that appeared earlier in the chapter. In an earlier article, Steve Savage argued that industrial farming is necessary to feed the world's population, and later we saw some of his research. Here, Halweil addresses some of Savage's claims as well as many other arguments that organic farming would require too much land and actually cause more problems than it solves. In the end, Halweil says the approach most likely to feed more people while doing less damage to the environment might be a middle ground between pure organic methods and conventional. Halweil is a senior researcher at Worldwatch and the author of the book Eat Here: Reclaiming Homegrown Pleasures in a Global Supermarket.

"Can Organic Farming Feed Us All?" by Brian Halweil, The Worldwatch Institute, November 2, 2016. Reprinted by permission.

As you read, consider the following questions:

1. What nations does Halweil say have the lowest gaps between yields of conventional and organic farming methods?

2. How, according to this article, is conventional farming harmful to biodiversity?

3. What is the "middle way" approach the author describes, and how would that help small farmers?

The only people who think organic farming can feed the world are delusional hippies, hysterical moms, and self-righteous organic farmers. Right?

Actually, no. A fair number of agribusiness executives, agricultural and ecological scientists, and international agriculture experts believe that a large-scale shift to organic farming would not only increase the world's food supply, but might be the only way to eradicate hunger.

This probably comes as a surprise. After all, organic farmers scorn the pesticides, synthetic fertilizers, and other tools that have become synonymous with high-yield agriculture. Instead, organic farmers depend on raising animals for manure, growing beans, clover, or other nitrogen-fixing legumes, or making compost and other sources of fertilizer that cannot be manufactured in a chemical plant but are instead grown-which consumes land, water, and other resources. (In contrast, producing synthetic fertilizers consumes massive amounts of petroleum.) Since organic farmers can't use synthetic pesticides, one can imagine that their fields suffer from a scourge of crop-munching bugs, fruit-rotting blights, and plant-choking weeds. And because organic farmers depend on rotating crops to help control pest problems, the same field won't grow corn or wheat or some other staple as often.

As a result, the argument goes, a world dependent on organic farming would have to farm more land than it does today—even if it meant less pollution, fewer abused farm animals, and fewer carcinogenic residues on our vegetables. "We aren't going to feed 6 billion people with organic fertilizer," said Nobel Prize-winning plant breeder Norman Borlaug at a 2002 conference. "If we tried to do it, we would level most of our forest and many of those lands would be productive only for a short period of time." Cambridge chemist John Emsley put it more bluntly: "The greatest catastrophe that the human race could face this century is not global warming but a global conversion to 'organic farming'-an estimated 2 billion people would perish."

In recent years, organic farming has attracted new scrutiny, not just from critics who fear that a large-scale shift in its direction would cause billions to starve, but also from farmers and development agencies who actually suspect that such a shift could better satisfy hungry populations. Unfortunately, no one had ever systematically analyzed whether in fact a widespread shift to organic farming would run up against a shortage of nutrients and a lack of yields-until recently. The results are striking.

High-Tech, Low-Impact

There are actually myriad studies from around the world showing that organic farms can produce about as much, and in some settings much more, than conventional farms. Where there is a yield gap, it tends to be widest in wealthy nations, where farmers use copious amounts of synthetic fertilizers and pesticides in a perennial attempt to maximize yields. It is true that farmers converting to organic production often encounter lower yields in the first few years, as the soil and surrounding biodiversity recover from years of assault with chemicals. And it may take several seasons for farmers to refine the new approach.

But the long-standing argument that organic farming would yield just one-third or one-half of conventional farming was based on biased assumptions and lack of data. For example, the often-cited statistic that switching to organic farming in the United States would only yield one-quarter of the food currently produced there is based on a U.S. Department of Agriculture study showing that all the manure in the United States could only meet one-quarter of the nation's fertilizer needs—even though organic farmers depend on much more than just manure.

More up-to-date research refutes these arguments. For example, a recent study by scientists at the Research Institute for Organic Agriculture in Switzerland showed that organic farms were only 20 percent less productive than conventional plots over a 21-year period. Looking at more than 200 studies in North America and Europe, Per Pinstrup Andersen (a Cornell professor and winner of the World Food Prize) and colleagues recently concluded that organic yields were about 80 percent of conventional yields. And many studies show an even narrower gap. Reviewing 154 growing seasons' worth of data on various crops grown on rain-fed and irrigated land in the United States, University of California-Davis agricultural scientist Bill Liebhardt found that organic corn yields were 94 percent of conventional yields, organic wheat yields were 97 percent, and organic soybean yields were 94 percent. Organic tomatoes showed no yield difference.

More importantly, in the world's poorer nations where most of the world's hungry live, the yield gaps completely disappear. University of Essex researchers Jules Pretty and Rachel Hine looked at over 200 agricultural projects in the developing world that converted to organic and ecological approaches, and found that for all the projects-involving 9 million farms on nearly 30 million hectares-yields increased an average of 93 percent. A seven-year study from Maikaal District in central India involving 1,000 farmers cultivating 3,200 hectares found that average yields for cotton, wheat, chili, and soy were as much as 20 percent higher on the organic farms than on nearby conventionally managed ones. Farmers and agricultural scientists attributed the higher yields in this dry region to the emphasis on cover crops, compost, manure, and other practices that increased organic matter (which helps retain water) in the soils. A study from Kenya found that while organic farmers in "high-potential areas" (those with above-average rainfall and high soil quality) had lower maize yields than nonorganic farmers, organic farmers in areas with poorer resource endowments consistently outyielded conventional growers. (In both regions, organic farmers had higher net profits, return on capital, and return on labor.)

Contrary to critics who jibe that it's going back to farming like our grandfathers did or that most of Africa already farms organically and it can't do the job, organic farming is a sophisticated combination of old wisdom and modern ecological innovations that help harness the yield-boosting effects of nutrient cycles, beneficial insects, and crop synergies. It's heavily dependent on technology-just not the technology that comes out of a chemical plant.

High-Calorie Farms

So could we make do without the chemical plants? Inspired by a field trip to a nearby organic farm where the farmer reported that he raised an amazing 27 tons of vegetables on six-tenths of a hectare in a relatively short growing season, a team of scientists from the University of Michigan tried to estimate how much food could be raised following a global shift to organic farming. The team combed through the literature for any and all studies comparing crop yields on organic farms with those on nonorganic farms. Based on 293 examples, they came up with a global dataset of yield ratios for the world's major crops for the developed and the developing world. As expected, organic farming yielded less than conventional farming in the developed world for most food categories, while studies from the developing world showed organic farming boosting yields. The team then ran two models. The first was conservative in the sense that it applied the yield ratio for the developed world to the entire planet, i.e., they assumed that every farm regardless of location would get only the lower developed-country yields. The second applied the yield ratio for the developed world to wealthy nations and the yield ratio for the developing world to those countries.

"We were all surprised by what we found," said Catherine Badgley, a Michigan paleoecologist who was one of the lead researchers. The first model yielded 2,641 kilocalories ("calories") per person per day, just under the world's current production of 2,786 calories but significantly higher than the average caloric requirement for a healthy person of between 2,200 and 2,500. The second model yielded 4,381 calories per person per day, 75 percent greater than current availability-and a quantity that could theoretically sustain a much larger human population than is currently supported on the world's farmland.

The team's interest in this subject was partly inspired by the concern that a large-scale shift to organic farming would require clearing additional wild areas to compensate for lower yields—an obvious worry for scientists like Badgley, who studies present and past biodiversity. The only problem with the argument, she said, is that much of the world's biodiversity exists in close proximity to farmland, and that's not likely to change anytime soon. "If we simply try to maintain biodiversity in islands around the world, we will lose most of it," she said. "It's very important to make areas between those islands friendly to biodiversity. The idea of those areas being pesticide-drenched fields is just going to be a disaster for biodiversity, especially in the tropics. The world would be able to sustain high levels of biodiversity much better if we could change agriculture on a large scale."

Badgley's team went out of the way to make its assumptions as conservative as possible: most of the studies they used looked at the yields of a single crop, even though many organic farms grow more than one crop in a field at the same time, yielding more total food even if the yield of any given crop may be lower. Skeptics may doubt the team's conclusions—as ecologists, they are likely to be sympathetic to organic farming—but a second recent study of the potential of a global shift to organic farming, led by Niels Halberg of the Danish Institute of Agricultural Sciences, came to very similar conclusions, even though the authors were economists, agronomists, and international development experts.

Like the Michigan team, Halberg's group made an assumption about the differences in yields with organic farming for a range of crops and then plugged those numbers into a model developed by the World Bank's International Food Policy Research Institute (IFPRI). This model is considered the definitive algorithm for predicting food output, farm income, and the number of hungry people throughout the world. Given the growing interest in organic farming among consumers, government officials, and agricultural scientists, the researchers wanted to assess whether a large-scale conversion to organic farming in Europe and North America (the world's primary food exporting regions) would reduce yields, increase world food prices, or worsen hunger in poorer nations that depend on imports, particularly those people living in the Third World's swelling megacities. Although the group found that total food production declined in Europe and North America, the model didn't show a substantial impact on world food prices. And because the model assumed, like the Michigan study, that organic farming would boost yields in Africa, Asia, and Latin America, the most optimistic scenario even had hunger-plagued sub-Saharan Africa exporting food surpluses.

"Modern non-certified organic farming is a potentially sustainable approach to agricultural development in areas with low yields due to poor access to inputs or low yield potential because it involves lower economic risk than comparative interventions based on purchased inputs and may increase farm level resilience against climatic fluctuations," Halberg's team concluded. In other words, studies from the field show that the yield increases from shifting to organic farming are highest and most consistent in exactly those poor, dry, remote areas where hunger is most severe. "Organic agriculture could be an important part of increased food security in sub-Saharan Africa," says Halberg.

That is, if other problems can be overcome. "A lot of research is to try to kill prejudices," Halberg says—like the notion that organic farming is only a luxury, and one that poorer nations cannot afford. "I'd like to kill this once and for all. The two sides are simply too far from each other and they ignore the realities of the global food system." Even if a shift toward organic farming boosted yields in hungry African and Asian nations, the model found that nearly a billion people remained hungry, because any surpluses were simply exported to areas that could best afford it.

Wrong Question?

These conclusions about yields won't come as a surprise to many organic farmers. They have seen with their own eyes and felt with their own hands how productive they can be. But some supporters of organic farming shy away from even asking whether it can feed the world, simply because they don't think it's the most useful question. There is good reason to believe that a global conversion to organic farming would not proceed as seamlessly as plugging some yield ratios into a spreadsheet.

To begin with, organic farming isn't as easy as farming with chemicals. Instead of choosing a pesticide to prevent a pest outbreak, for example, a particular organic farmer might consider altering his crop rotation, planting a crop that will repel the pest or one that will attract its predators—decisions that require some experimentation and long-term planning. Moreover, the IFPRI study suggested that a large-scale conversion to organic farming might require that most dairy and beef production eventually "be better integrated in cereal and other cash crop rotations" to optimize use of the manure. Bringing cows back to one or two farms to build up soil fertility may seem like a no-brainer, but doing it wholesale would be a challenge—and dumping ammonia on depleted soils still makes for a quicker fix.

Again, these are just theoretical assumptions, since a global shift to organic farming could take decades. But farmers are ingenious and industrious people and they tend to cope with whatever problems are at hand. Eliminate nitrogen fertilizer and many farmers will probably graze cows on their fields to compensate. Eliminate fungicides and farmers will look for fungus-resistant crop varieties. As more and more farmers begin to farm organically, everyone will get better at it. Agricultural research centers, universities, and agriculture ministries will throw their resources into this type of farming—in sharp contrast to their current neglect of organic agriculture, which partly stems from the assumption that organic farmers will never play a major role in the global food supply.

So the problems of adopting organic techniques do not seem insurmountable. But those problems may not deserve most of our attention; even if a mass conversion over, say, the next two decades, dramatically increased food production, there's little guarantee it would eradicate hunger. The global food system can be a complex and unpredictable beast. It's hard to anticipate how China's rise as a major importer of soybeans for its feedlots, for instance, might affect food supplies elsewhere. (It's likely to drive up food prices.) Or how elimination of agricultural subsidies in wealthy nations might affect poorer countries. (It's likely to boost farm incomes and reduce hunger.) And would less meat eating around the world free up food for the hungry? (It would, but could the hungry afford it?) In other words, "Can organic farming feed the world?" is probably not even the right question, since feeding the world depends more on politics and economics than any technological innovations.

"'Can organic farming feed the world' is indeed a bogus question," says Gene Kahn, a long-time organic farmer who founded Cascadian Farms organic foods and is now vice president of sustainable development for General Mills. "The real question is, can we feed the world? Period. Can we fix the disparities in human nutrition?" Kahn notes that the marginal difference in today's organic yields and the yields of conventional agriculture wouldn't matter if food surpluses were redistributed.

But organic farming will yield other benefits that are too numerous to name. Studies have shown, for example, that the "external" costs of organic farming—erosion, chemical pollution to drinking water, death of birds and other wildlife—are just one-third those of conventional farming. Surveys from every continent show that organic farms support many more species of birds, wild plants, insects, and other wildlife than conventional farms. And tests by several governments have shown that organic foods carry just a tiny fraction of the pesticide residues of the nonorganic alternatives, while completely banning growth hormones, antibiotics, and many additives allowed in many conventional foods. There is even some evidence that crops grown organically have considerably higher levels of health-promoting antioxidants.

There are social benefits as well. Because organic farming doesn't depend on expensive inputs, it might help shift the balance towards smaller farmers in hungry nations. A 2002 report from the UN Food and Agriculture Organization noted that "organic systems can double or triple the productivity of traditional systems" in developing nations but suggested that yield comparisons offer a "limited, narrow, and often misleading picture" since farmers in these countries often adopt organic farming techniques to save water, save money, and reduce the variability of yields in extreme conditions. A more recent study by the International Fund for Agricultural Development found that the higher labor requirements often mean that "organic agriculture can prove particularly effective in bringing redistribution of resources in areas where the labour force is underemployed. This can help contribute to rural stability."

Middle Earth

These benefits will come even without a complete conversion to a sort of organic utopia. In fact, some experts think that a more hopeful, and reasonable, way forward is a sort of middle ground, where more and more farmers adopt the principles of organic farming even if they don't follow the approach religiously. In this scenario, both poor farmers and the environment come out way ahead. "Organic agriculture is not going to do the trick," says Roland Bunch, an agricultural extensionist who has worked for decades in Africa and the Americas and is now with COSECHA (Association of Consultants for a Sustainable, Ecological, and People-Centered Agriculture) in Honduras. Bunch knows first-hand that organic agriculture can produce more than conventional farming among poorer farmers. But he also knows that these farmers cannot get the premium prices paid for organic produce elsewhere, and that they are often unable, and unwilling, to shoulder some of the costs and risks associated with going completely organic.

Instead, Bunch points to "a middle path," of eco-agriculture, or low-input agriculture that uses many of the principles of organic farming and depends on just a small fraction of the chemicals. "These systems can immediately produce two or three times what smallholder farmers are presently producing," Bunch says. "And furthermore, it is attractive to smallholder farmers because it is less costly per unit produced." In addition to the immediate gains in food production, Bunch suggests that the benefits for the environment of this middle path will be far greater than going "totally organic," because "something like five to ten times as many smallholder farmers will adopt it per unit of extension and training expense, because it behooves them economically. They aren't taking food out of their kids' mouths. If five farmers eliminate half their use of chemicals, the effect on the environment will be two and one-half times as great as if one farmer goes totally organic."

And farmers who focus on building their soils, increasing biodiversity, or bringing livestock into their rotation aren't precluded from occasionally turning to biotech crops or synthetic nitrogen or any other yield-enhancing innovations in the future, particularly in places where the soils are heavily depleted. "In the end, if we do things right, we'll build a lot of organic into conventional systems," says Don Lotter, the agricultural consultant. Like Bunch, Lotter notes that such an "integrated" approach often out-performs both a strictly organic and chemical-intensive approach in terms of yield, economics, and environmental benefits. Still, Lotter's not sure we'll get there tomorrow, since the world's farming is hardly pointed in the organic direction—which could be the real problem for the world's poor and hungry. "There is such a huge area in sub-Saharan Africa and South America where the Green Revolution has never made an impact and it's unlikely that it will for the next generation of poor farmers," argues Niels Halberg, the Danish scientist who lead the IFPRI study. "It seems that agro-ecological measures for some of these areas have a beneficial impact on yields and food insecurity. So why not seriously try it out?"

Periodical and Internet Sources Bibliography

The following articles have been selected to supplement the diverse views presented in this chapter.

Catherine Badly and Steve Savage, "Can Organic Food Feed the World?" *Wall Street Journal*, July 12, 2015. http://www.wsj.com /articles/can-organic-food-feed-the-world-1436757046.

David Biello, "Will Organic Food Fail to Feed the World?" *Scientific American*, April 25, 2012. https://www.scientificamerican.com /article/organic-farming-yields-and-feeding-the-world-under -climate-change.

Mark Bittman, "Don't Ask How to Feed the 9 Billion," *New York Times*, November 11, 2014. https://www.nytimes.com /2014/11/12/opinion/dont-ask-how-to-feed-the-9-billion.html.

Norman Borlaug, "We Need Biotech to Feed the World," *Wall Street Journal*, December 6, 2000.

Jonathan Foley, "A Five Step Plan to Feed the World," *National Geographic*. http://www.nationalgeographic.com/foodfeatures /feeding-9-billion.

Beth Gardiner, "A Roadmap for Eradicating World Hunger," *New York Times*, June 24,2015. http://www.nytimes.com/2015/06/25 /business/energy-environment/food-tomorrow-hope-for -eradicating-world-hunger.html?_r=0.

Tom Philpott, "Does Corporate Farming Exist? Barely," *Mother Jones*, September 25, 2013. http://www.motherjones.com/tom -philpott/2013/09/does-corporate-farming-exist-barely.

Tom Philpott, "No Giant Farms Are Not Feeding the World. They're Feeding Canada," *Mother Jones*, October 5, 2016. http://www .motherjones.com/environment/2016/10/charts-our-industrial -scale-farms-dont-feed-worlds-hungry.

Michael Pollan, "How to Feed the World," *Newsweek*, May 19, 2008. http://michaelpollan.com/articles-archive/how-to-feed-the -world.

Jenny Purt, "Feeding the World: How on Earth Can We Feed Nine Billion People?" *Guardian*, June 21, 2012. https://www .theguardian.com/sustainable-business/feeding-world-nine -billion-population.

John Vidal, "Corporate Stranglehold of Farmland a Risk to World Food Security, Study Says," *Guardian*, May 28, 2014. https://www .theguardian.com/environment/2014/may/28/farmland-food -security-small-farmers.

OPPOSING
VIEWPOINTS®
SERIES

CHAPTER 2

Is Corporate Farming Environmentally Sustainable?

Chapter Preface

In January 2015, between 25,000 and 50,000 people (depending on whether you take the estimates of the organizers or the police) took to the streets of Berlin, Germany, united by the motto "We Are Sick of Agribusiness." They marched in protest calling for an end to mega-factory farms and the genetic manipulation of food. Though this was a particularly large and well-organized protest (more than 120 environmental, consumer, and development organizations were involved in the event), it was not an anomaly. People all over the industrialized world are beginning to question the wisdom of modern corporate, industrial farming techniques.

While many voices debate the feasibility of feeding ten billion people using solely organic methods, these protestors say that there is no other option—at least not if we want the planet to remain habitable much longer for any of those ten billion people. In the quest for greater and greater yields, industrial farming has, say its critics, depleted the soil of nutrients, dangerously depleted aquifers, spewed poisons into both air and water, reduced the amount of biodiversity on the planet, and contributed significantly to global warming. And the potential dangers of genetically modified crops are still being explored.

Surprisingly, you'll find few who attempt to argue that industrial farming is good for the environment. However, there are specific issues on which the industrial farming community pushes back against environmentalists who claim that modern corporate farming is wrecking the planet. There have been many arguments that genetically modified seed and crops are safe, and some that argue that the dangers of pesticides have been overblown. Often the arguments come down to numbers—not *if* there is a problem, but just *how bad* the problem is, and whether alternative farming methods can solve these problems while still feeding the world. A risk-benefit analysis, say supporters of agribusiness, suggests that the risks of high-tech, consolidated farming are worth taking if we are to prevent increased hunger worldwide.

In the following chapter, you will read articles arguing that genetically modified crops are safe, that America's obsession with corn products is not only killing the environment but the people who live in it as well, that modern agricultural practices are the main driver of global warming, and a few articles that offer solutions to the potential conflict between feeding the world and poisoning it.

> *"The monomania of corn production utterly disregards economic, environmental and social concerns."*

America's Political Commitment to Producing Corn at the Expense of Other Crops Damages the Environment

Bill Hewitt

In the following viewpoint, Bill Hewitt argues that American agriculture is dangerously fixated on one monoculture in particular: corn. (A monoculture is generally defined as the practice of producing one single crop.) Hewitt cites sources that point out the economic and political reasons for this enormous emphasis on just one crop, the hazards that it poses to the environment, and the damage it does to the health of the population. He closes by suggesting ways to reduce the emphasis on corn. Bill Hewitt is a writer, environmental professional, and activist who teaches at New York University's Center for Global Affairs and is the author of A Newer World: Politics, Money, Technology, and What's Really Being Done to Solve the Climate Crisis.

"Six Problems with Monoculture Farming," Open Permaculture School with "Monoculture Mania Must and Can Be Overcome," by Bill Hewitt, Our World, August 20, 2012. https://ourworld.unu.edu/en/monoculture-mania-must-and-can-be-overcome.

As you read, consider the following questions:

1. How does Hewitt define "monomania" as it applies to American farming?

2. According to Hewitt, how does climate change affect agriculture?

3. What is one way Hewitt suggests limiting our dependence on corn?

By monoculture, I don't just mean the production of one crop over vast quantities of land, with all the resultant havoc that such practice plays on the soil, water, native flora and fauna, and, to be perfectly clear, on the climate system, but I also mean the monomania that is incarnate in Big Ag.

Monomania is a serious disorder, characterized by, according to my dictionary, "excessive concentration on a single object or idea." In the case of much of American farming, that single object is the production of as much corn as possible at the greatest possible return on investment. The monomania of corn production utterly disregards economic, environmental and social concerns.

The word itself is, to be sure, old-fashioned, but it is nevertheless manifest in how modern society goes about the business of growing our food, feed and, most wastefully of all, our fuel.

Does industrial agriculture stress our precious freshwater supplies? You bet it does. You think the Aral Sea disaster can't happen where you live? A new paper published in *Nature* reports that "…humans are overexploiting groundwater in many large aquifers that are critical to agriculture, especially in Asia and North America".

Does the massive over-application of nitrogen fertilizer and subsequent runoff cause marine dead zones all over the world? Right again. Here's an irony while we're on the subject: The drought this year in the American corn belt has minimized the amount of fertilizer runoff such that the dead zone in the Gulf of Mexico is the smallest it's been in years.

Does the use of fertilizer exacerbate climate change? You got it. Do chemical fertilizers and manure threaten drinking water? Yes. By the way, for a really superb experience of documentary filmmaking that will open your eyes to the realities of industrial agriculture and the many, diverse and proven ways to farm sustainably—and more productively—see *Dirt! The Movie*.

So, to the heat and the drought. As you know well by now, July was the hottest month on record for the lower 48 US states.

"The average temperature for the contiguous US during July was 77.6°F [25°C], 3.3°F above the 20th century average, marking the warmest July and all-time warmest month on record for the nation in a period of record that dates back to 1895," the US National Climatic Data Center reported.

Think this is all an aberration? Think again. The United States Department of Agriculture, will tell you, point blank, that climate change is here and it has consequences for agriculture, including that "increasing temperatures will increase the risk of crop failures, particularly if precipitation decreases or becomes more variable."

There have been two eminently sane op-eds in the *NY Times* recently about corn, heat and the drought. The first, "Corn for Food, Not Fuel," reminds us of the sobering fact that 40 percent of the US corn crop is simply feedstock for ethanol. The use of ethanol, maddeningly, is mandated by law. It's supposed to help reduce American dependence on foreign oil. But it exacerbates air pollution, reduces engine efficiency and is a net contributor to climate change, wrecks engines, crowds out farming of other food crops, and distorts prices for grains.

As the always excellent *Christian Science Monitor* reports here, the alarm bells are ringing all over the world now on food prices. We've seen this movie before. Over four years ago, we were warned about how biofuel production was driving up food prices.

Paul Krugman [Nobel Prize winning economist], among others, including ten of the country's top environmental scientists, said then that our ethanol policies were folly. Krugman, eloquent and pithy, said in his column "...land used to grow biofuel feedstock is land not available to grow food, so subsidies to biofuels are a major factor in the food crisis. You might put it this way: people are starving in Africa so that American politicians can court votes in farm states."

Some politicians—not from corn-producing states (surprise, surprise)—have called on the EPA to waive the requirement for ethanol. This would allow us to devote more of the corn that's left from this year's devastated crop to be used for food, alleviating the concerns over prices.

Beyond this simple, reasonable and rational measure, we can and should be doing more to reduce our dependence on the corn monoculture. The other clear-headed *NY Times* op-ed, "The Silver Lining in the Drought," calls for us to change course in a number of other ways: reduce farm subsidies (first and most importantly), recreate the diversity of American farming, and move to a "a rebalancing of the food system from a few megaproducers and lots of importers to a more decentralized mix."

I would add that we need to reduce our use of corn for livestock—indeed radically reduce our consumption of meat—and stop sweetening virtually every processed food with high fructose corn syrup. We have an obesity epidemic in this country. We need to rethink what we eat altogether.

I tell people I've been a vegetarian for 41 of my 60 years and I'm going pretty darn strong. It's not hard to do. It's pretty easy. Get informed, in any event, about food and agriculture. It's not only about your health but it's about the future of the planet and our companions on Spaceship Earth. As Captain Picard would say: "Make it so."

> *"Industrial agriculture contributes significantly to climate change and it depends on a resource that won't always be there. We have to move to a modern, low input, sustainable agriculture."*

Modern Industrial Agriculture Is Destroying the Ecosystem

Peter Saunders

Throughout this text, authors tend to use the phrases "industrial farming" and "corporate farming" more or less interchangeably. In the following viewpoint, Peter Saunders, in an address to the European Parliament, explains what industrial farming really is and how it is expanding, before going on to detail some of the potentially catastrophic effects on the environment if we do not change course. He goes on to explain why agricultural corporations are not willing to support ecologically responsible farming methods. Saunders is emeritus professor at Kings College, Strand campus.

"Industrial Agriculture and Global Warming," by Peter Saunders, Independent Science Panel, October 20, 2004 (http://www.i-sis.org.uk/isp/IAGW.php). Reprinted by permission.

As you read, consider the following questions:

1. Why does Saunders say that dwindling supplies of oil will require new farming methods?

2. According to Saunders, what role does positive feedback play in the effects of global warming?

3. How might global warming actually make it colder in northern Europe?

We all imagine farming as being very different from industry. One consists of pastures green and fields of golden corn, the other of dark satanic mills belching smoke into the sky. But farming is becoming industrialised. In developed countries, and more and more in the third world as well, traditional agriculture is being replaced by new methods that require large inputs of fertilisers, herbicides and pesticides, that depend on large scale irrigation, and that consume large quantities of fuel both in growing the food and in delivering it to consumers who may be thousands of miles away.

Now we can't go on like this, for at least two reasons. First, the world's supply of oil is drying up. It's obviously hard to say exactly how long it will last, but estimates from experts including British Petroleum and OPEC suggest between 25 and 50 years. More oil fields may be found, or we may get better at extracting it from existing fields, but that's the scale of the problem. And we can't assume that the third world will continue to use so much less than we do.

Even if we find more oil, there remains the problem of global warming. As I'm sure you know, there is now a consensus among almost all the experts in the field that over the 21st century the mean temperature of the Earth will rise by no less than 2 C and possibly as much as 5.8 C.

And as the models are improved, that top figure itself is being revised upwards. The Hadley Centre in the UK now estimates that the rise might be as much as 8 C, and the difference is that they have been taking into account the effect of changes in vegetation, both through the destruction of the rain forests (with the accompanying release of carbon into the atmosphere) and through changes in vegetation caused by the global warming itself.

That last is very important, by the way, because it's an example of what is known in control theory as positive feedback. A rise in the Earth's temperature leads to a change in vegetation, for example the loss of rain forests that hold water and carbon. This leads to a rise in temperature, which changes the vegetation even further, and so on. You might ask where this ends, and the answer is that nobody knows. But the US National Research Council was sufficiently concerned that they commissioned a Committee on Abrupt Climate Change, and their report, published a couple of years ago, is not reassuring.

There have certainly been abrupt climate changes in the past. At the end of a period called the Younger Dryas, about 11,500 years ago, there was a sudden rise in temperature over most of the Earth. The only really accurate data we have are from ice cores in Greenland, and there the temperature went up by 8 C in a decade. That's right—a decade, not a century.

And if you think a bit of global warming might be nice for those of us who live in Northern Europe, I'd just remind you that one expected consequence would be the switching off of the Gulf Stream, which is what keeps us as warm as we are. The reason is that if the Arctic and Greenland ice sheets melt, the surface water in the North Atlantic would become less salty and wouldn't sink as it cools, making it like the North Pacific where there is no similar warming current. The ice sheets are melting and the North Atlantic is becoming less salty, so there's another warning.

The Intergovernmental Panel on Climate Change says we can expect a considerable increase in heat waves, storms, floods, and the spread of tropical diseases into temperate areas. It also predicts a rise in sea levels up to eighty-eight centimetres this century, which will affect (by seawater intrusion into the soils underlying croplands and by temporary and also permanent flooding) something like 30% of the world's agricultural lands. Things are getting serious.

Agriculture inevitably makes a contribution to greenhouse gases, as does just about every human activity. You and I breathe out carbon dioxide all the time. But the effect of modern industrial agriculture is very much greater. Currently it is responsible for 25% of the world's carbon dioxide emissions, 60% of methane gas emissions and 80% of nitrous oxide. It's going to be hard to get fossil fuel consumption down, and agriculture has an important contribution to make which need not compromise our food supply.

The most energy-intensive components of modern industrial agriculture are the production of nitrogen fertiliser, farm machinery and pumped irrigation. They account for more than 90% of the total direct and indirect energy used in agriculture and are essential to it. It has been estimated that to produce a tonne of cereals or vegetables by means of modern agriculture requires 6 to 10 times more energy than by using sustainable agricultural methods.

Through the action of denitrifying soil bacteria, land conversion is leading to the release of around half a million tonnes a year of nitrogen in the form of nitrous oxide. Nitrous oxide is up to 300 times more potent than carbon dioxide as a greenhouse gas, though fortunately atmospheric concentrations of nitrous oxide are currently less than one-thousandth that of carbon dioxide. Around 70 million tonnes a year of nitrogen are now applied to crops, contributing as much as 10% of the total annual nitrous oxide emissions of 22 million tonnes. With fertiliser applications increasing substantially, especially in developing countries, nitrous oxide emissions from agriculture could double over the next 30 years.

The growth of agriculture is also leading to increasing emissions of methane. We are raising far more cattle, often on land which was once covered with forests, and we are feeding them on a high protein diet, which makes them emit even more methane than do grass-fed cattle. Even the fertilisation of grasslands with nitrogen

INDUSTRIAL AGRICULTURE IS NOT THE MIRACLE IT WAS SOLD TO BE

Industrial agriculture is currently the dominant food production system in the United States. It's characterized by large-scale monoculture, heavy use of chemical fertilizers and pesticides, and meat production in CAFOs (confined animal feeding operations). The industrial approach to farming is also defined by its heavy emphasis on a few crops that overwhelmingly end up as animal feed, biofuels, and processed junk food ingredients.

From its mid-20th century beginnings, industrial agriculture has been sold to the public as a technological miracle. Its efficiency, we were told, would allow food production to keep pace with a rapidly growing global population, while its economies of scale would ensure that farming remained a profitable business.

But too often, something crucial was left out of this story: the price tag.

In fact, our industrialized food and agriculture system comes with steep costs, many of which are picked up by taxpayers, rural communities, farmers themselves, other business sectors, and future generations. When we include these "externalities" in our reckoning, we can see that this system is not a cost-effective, healthful, or sustainable way to produce the food we need.

And the good news is that it's not the only way. Scientists and farmers are developing smart, modern agricultural systems that could reduce or eliminate many of the costs of industrial agriculture—and still allow farmers to run a profitable business. It's time for farm policy to move into the 21st century and prioritize these innovative methods.

"Hidden Costs of Industrial Agriculture," Union of Concerned Scientists (www. UCSUSA.org).

fertilisers can both decrease methane uptake by soil bacteria and increase nitrous oxide production, thereby increasing atmospheric concentrations of both these gases. The expansion of rice paddies has also seriously increased methane emissions. Rain-fed rice produces far less methane than inundated rice fertilised with nitrogen fertiliser.

We are now encountering diminishing returns on fertilisers. The Food and Agricultural Organisation of the United Nations (FAO) admitted in 1997 that wheat yields in both Mexico and the USA had shown no increase in 13 years. In 1999, global wheat production actually fell for the second consecutive year to about 589 million tons, down 2% from 1998. Overuse of fertilisers also renders the soil less fertile in the long run, so that fertilisers become less effective.

Pesticides too are becoming less effective. Weeds, fungi, insects and other potential pests are amazingly adaptable. Five hundred species of insects have already developed genetic resistance to pesticides, as have 150 plant diseases, 133 kinds of weeds and 70 species of fungus. The reaction today is to apply ever more powerful and more expensive poisons, but this is inevitably a losing battle.

Nor is the answer genetic modification, which we are constantly being told has the potential to transform agriculture. Mind you, the lobbyists always talk about the potential, not real accomplishments, and at least in the UK we are told that we need it not so we can have a secure food supply, but in case someone else gets in first and we fall behind in the agrochemical business.

Genetically modified crops, contrary to what we are told, do not increase yields. They require more inputs, including more herbicides, whose use they are supposed to reduce significantly. They lead to profits, but only for the manufacturers, not for the farmers and certainly not for the consumers.

And they pose dangers which have never been properly assessed, largely because the only organisations with the resources to assess them properly do not consider it to be in their interests to carry out the work. No one knows for sure what will be consequences of introducing, by a very crude technique, a specific gene (or rather a specific piece of DNA, which is not the same thing) into the genome of a very different creature. It's something we should certainly be trying to find out—but not by rushing transgenic crops into production and letting the genes loose in the environment.

The problems that GM solves are often merely consequences of industrial agriculture anyway. Let me give you one example. In Southeast Asia, where rice is the staple crop, they have been genetically modifying rice to be resistant to bacterial blight. On the face of it, that sounds like an advance. But while bacterial blight has been around for a long time, it's only recently become a serious problem. When you grow rice in the traditional way, in small paddy fields alongside other crops, and with each village growing a slightly different variety, you may get an occasional outbreak, but it won't spread. Industrial agriculture means you use large fields, you don't intercrop, and you grow a single variety of rice throughout a large region. Just the conditions in which bacterial blight and all sorts of other nasties can prosper.

What is more, they had trouble finding a variety of rice from which they could isolate the gene they wanted, so if bacterial blight becomes resistant, they'll be no further ahead, and the result could be disaster for the farmers and the people who depend on them.

We must not throw away the knowledge and experience that has been accumulated by millions of farmers over several thousand years. But we can go beyond what they have learned because we have modern science to help us. If only a fraction of the money being devoted to developing GM crops were spent on improving traditional methods, think how much progress we could make.

Why don't we? Well, first of all, we are. There is work being done and it is succeeding. Just to cite one example, it's been shown that you don't have to genetically modify sweet potatoes to make them pest resistant; you only have to adapt an intercropping system that's traditionally been used in parts of Africa. Naturally the GM lobby claimed it wouldn't work in South Africa, but it does.

But because that sort of research doesn't lead to patents, companies aren't going to do it. Even universities and government laboratories are less keen than they used to be on carrying out work that won't generate royalties for them. And, unusually, GM allows companies actually to own and control varieties, so there is a big incentive to do by GM what you might have done by other, less hazardous, means.

We are told that industrial agriculture is efficient, by which is meant that it produces crops for less money. Well, I don't know how the sums work out if you add in the hidden costs like degradation of land, pollution of rivers, and so on. But even if the claim is correct, think how the efficiency comes about. Industrial agriculture is less labour intensive, but it relies heavily on oil and oil products. Now just about everyone agrees we are going to run out of oil; the only question is when. I haven't heard anybody say there is a shortage of human beings on the planet. What sort of efficiency is it that arises by replacing a resource that we have lots of by one that is rapidly being exhausted?

Industrial agriculture contributes significantly to climate change and it depends on a resource that won't always be there. We have to move to a modern, low input, sustainable agriculture. And the proper role of science is to help us achieve this, not to make a fast buck for a few biotech companies.

> *"What evidence will it take to convince the public that GM foods are as safe as non-GM foods?"*

The Scientific Debate About GM Foods Is Over: They're Safe

Michael White

In the following viewpoint, Michael White points out that the scientific consensus is that genetically modified crops are safe for the environment (as well as for consumption), but the public is unwilling to accept this evidence. One reason, he argues, is that companies that make GMOs have not made a clear case why GMOs are of a benefit to consumers. As we saw in the previous viewpoint (and shall see again in Chapter Four) consumers are concerned that the people saying GMOs are safe can't be trusted because they have financial interests in the outcome of the debate. White says we need better systems for assuring the public that decisions about how to grow foods are not based solely on corporate profits. White is an assistant professor of genetics at Washington University in St. Louis, Missouri.

As you read, consider the following questions:

1. How might scientists do a better job of getting the public to trust their research?

2. White mentions non-GMO modified crops created by modern breeding programs. What kinds of breeding programs do you think he is talking about?

3. What problems, according to White, are scientists who work on GMO foods trying to solve?

It's no secret that people are nervous about foods made from genetically modified organisms. A July Gallup poll found that 48 percent of respondents believed that GM foods "pose a serious health hazard," compared to 36 percent who didn't. California voters may have rejected a ballot initiative to require labeling of GM foods last fall, but a *New York Times* survey found overwhelming support for mandatory labeling on the packaging of GM foods.

Within the scientific community, the debate over the safety of GM foods is over. The overwhelming conclusion is, in the words of the American Association for the Advancement of Science, that "consuming foods containing ingredients derived from GM crops is no riskier than consuming the same foods containing ingredients from crop plants modified by conventional plant improvement techniques." Major scientific and governmental organizations agree. The U.S. National Academy of Sciences found that "no adverse health effects attributed to genetic engineering have been documented in the human population," and a report issued by the European Commission made the same claim. The World Health Organization has concluded that GM foods "are not likely, nor have been shown, to present risks for human health."

What evidence will it take to convince the public that GM foods are as safe as non-GM foods?

The scientific literature backs this up. In February, the *Journal of Agricultural and Food Chemistry* published a literature review covering 20 years of safety studies. The authors found "overwhelming evidence" that using biotechnology to genetically modify crops "is less disruptive of crop composition compared with traditional breeding, which itself has a tremendous history of safety." An overview of safety studies appearing this month in *Nature Biotechnology* noted that, despite disagreement over a need for more long-term safety studies, both critics and proponents of GMOs agree that so far "genetically modified foods have failed to produce any untoward health effects."

In other words, the scientific consensus is that GMOs do not pose risks to our health or the environment that are any different from the risks posed by the non-GM crops created with modern breeding programs.

The discrepancy between the public debate over GM foods and the debate within the scientific community has left many scientists puzzling over the question: What evidence will it take to convince the public that GM foods are as safe as non-GM foods?

The editors at *Nature Biotechnology* argue that evidence is not the problem. The issue is that, so far, people have no reason to believe GM foods are being created for their benefit. Changing negative attitudes will "require a concerted and long-term effort to develop GM foods that clearly provide convincing benefits to consumers—something that seed companies have conspicuously failed to do over the past decade." The question of benefits has been buried because the GMO debate has been framed around the unhelpful distinction between GM and non-GM foods. Instead of asking if GM foods in general are less safe, the editors argue, we should be focused on the specific risks and benefits of individual products, whether they are GM or not.

A focus on the risks and benefits of all new crops could move the debate in a direction that would prompt scientists, companies, and regulators to more clearly justify the role GMOs play in our food supply. To date, consumers nervous about GMOs have been given little reason to think that companies like Monsanto are designing GM crops to solve any problem other than the one of patents and profits. As journalist Mark Lynas put it in his rousing defense of GM foods, for most people GMOs are about a "big American corporation with a nasty track record, putting something new and experimental into our food without telling us."

But many researchers working on GM crops are in fact trying to solve important problems, such as feeding a growing population, keeping food prices affordable worldwide, making healthier fruits and vegetables widely available, confronting the challenging growing conditions of a changing climate, saving Florida's oranges or Hawaii's papaya from pests, and fighting malnourishment in the developing world. For many of these problems, genetic engineering is faster, more cost-effective, and more reliable than conventional breeding methods.

Our society's unresolved controversy over GMOs is not about safety; it's about whether we have an acceptable process in place to ensure that our health is not put at risk for the sake of biotech's bottom line. Researchers, biotech companies, and regulators need to settle on an appropriately rigorous, transparent, and independent safety testing process for all new crops, one whose methods and results are publicly available. Currently, as the *Nature Biotechnology* review notes, safety assessments in the U.S. are a patchwork affair with weak legal underpinnings. But for GM solutions to our food challenges to be widely accepted, the public needs to know that they are not being coerced into eating something whose risks and benefits are unknown.

> "We are living in a very polluted and dangerous food world, partly because of the unregulated excesses of U.S. industrial farming."

Factory Farming Needs More Government Regulation

Will Allen

In the following viewpoint, Will Allen argues that lack of regulation of the agricultural industry is as much of a risk to the environment and human health as lack of regulation of the financial industry is to the economy. This piece was written in 2009, shortly after Barack Obama became president of the United States—and right after the onset of a serious financial crisis caused by lack of regulation on Wall Street. Allen uses data on pesticide use that he collected when writing his book The War on Bugs *to make a case for more regulation of pesticide use. Though the data here is slightly out of date, the basics have not changed. Allen has been farming organically since 1972 in Oregon, California, and Vermont, where he now co-manages Cedar Circle Farm.*

As you read, consider the following questions:

1. Why does Allen say that current regulations aren't effective?

2. What "war chemicals" does Allen say can be found in the US drinking water supply?

3. In what way is the word "conventional" a semantic ploy, according to Allen?

Industrial ag supplies most of our food, yet its lack of regulation may be more of a threat than Wall Street's.

Taxpayers are demanding that government enforce existing regulations and create more stringent rules to limit the excess and greed in banking, insurance, housing, and on Wall Street. But, in the rush to regulate, we can't forget to oversee industrial agriculture. It is one of our most polluting and dangerous industries. Like the financial sectors, its practices have not been well regulated for the last thirty years. Let me run down a few of the major problems that have developed because of our poorly regulated U.S. agriculture.

Carbon Foot Print: The U.S. EPA estimated in 2007 that agriculture in the U.S. was responsible for about 18% of our carbon footprint, which is huge because the U.S. is the largest polluter in the world. This should include (but doesn't) the manufacture and use of pesticides and fertilizers, fuel and oil for tractors, equipment, trucking and shipping, electricity for lighting, cooling, and heating, and emissions of carbon dioxide, methane, nitrous oxide and other green house gases. Unfortunately, the EPA estimate of 18% still doesn't include a large portion of the fuel, the synthetic nitrogen fertilizer, some of the nitrous oxide, all of the CFCs and bromines, and most of the transport emissions. When they are counted, agriculture's share of the U.S. carbon footprint will be at least 25 to 30%.

Oftentimes we see all greenhouse gasses as being equivalent to carbon dioxide (CO_2). But, methane emissions are 21 times and nitrous oxides 310 times more damaging as greenhouse gasses than

CO2. Since agriculture is one of the largest producers of methane and nitrous oxide, the extent of the agricultural impact is staggering. Unless we change our bad habits of food production and long distance delivery, we will not be able to deal with climate change.

Fertilizer Pollution/Dead Zones: Factory farming is polluting the ground, river, and ocean water with high amounts of nitrogen, phosphorous, and other fertilizers. High levels of nitrates and nitrites were found in twenty-five thousand community wells that provided drinking water to two thirds of the nation's population. More than fifteen million people in two hundred eighty communities are drinking water with phosphorous or phosphates which mostly come from industrial farming operations.

Nitrate and phosphorous fertilizer runoff flow into the rivers and ultimately end up in the ocean. The river water rides up over the heavier salt water when it reaches the ocean and algae blooms develop on the fertilizer rich water. When the algae die, the bacteria use up all of the oxygen in decomposing them. This creates an oxygen dead (or hypoxic) zone. In 1995, scientists identified 60 dead zones around the world.

Recent results published in 2008 identified 405 oceanic dead zones. The prime cause for dead zones is the use of highly soluble synthetic fertilizers, which are overused to obtain maximum yields. The government regulations on the total maximum daily load (tmdl) of synthetic nitrogen, or phosphorous fertilizer coming off of farms were established under the Clean Water Act. But those statutes are routinely not enforced. There are exceptions, but in general the regulators have been in a thirty-year coma.

Pesticides in Water: In addition to fertilizer pollution of our food and water, high amounts of pesticides, antibiotics, and hormones are also in the food, soil, water, and air. More than twelve thousand wells that provide water to 100 million people have arsenic or lead concentrations above the health based limits established by the U.S.EPA. Arsenic has been used on crops in the U.S. since 1867 and lead-arsenic since 1890. Arsenic is still widely used today on turf crops, corn, soy, and cotton as an herbicide or defoliant. The EPA, FDA, USDA and almost all state agencies, however, do not even keep good track of arsenic use. It is hard to regulate when you don't know how much is being used.

While we don't know how much was used, we do know that nearly 30 million people in the U.S. are drinking water contaminated with Atrazine, Simazine, Telone II, 2,4-D, or 2,4,5-T. All of these chemicals are related to DDT and were first sold in the 1940s, after they were developed in World War II. Simazine and 2,4,5-T had their EPA registrations cancelled more than twenty years ago because they were so deadly; yet millions of people in the U.S. still drink water contaminated with these two terrible war toys. All these DDT relatives caused cancer and multiple birth defects in tests on laboratory animals. They continue today to greatly damage bird populations in farm country.

Two of these war materials, 2,4-D, and 2,4,5-T along with Dioxin were the poisons in Agent Orange, the defoliant that killed and crippled so many Vietnamese and American soldiers and turned jungle into denuded ghost lands. Somehow, the officials at EPA and FDA seem to think that it is OK for millions of U.S. citizens to have these two killer chemicals in their drinking water.

Excessive Pesticide Use Today: Factory farmers continue to use enormous quantities of the most toxic poisons. In 2006, four of the six most used farm pesticides in California were among the most dangerous chemicals in the world. Farmers applied more than 35.7 million pounds of four pesticides: Metam sodium, Methyl bromide, Telone II, and Chloropicrin.

Metam sodium, the third most used California pesticide in 2006, is closely related to the chemical gas that escaped in Bhopal India in 1984 and killed 30,000 people and injured 200,000. Fourteen million, eight hundred thousand pounds were used in California in 2006. Metam sodium is a biocide, causes multiple birth defects, farmworker injuries, and is very toxic to birds and fish.

In 2006, California farmers used seven million pounds of Methyl bromide, the fourth most used farm pesticide in the state, and the notorious destroyer of the ozone. The EPA registration for Methyl bromide was scheduled for cancellation in 1995 as a result of Montreal Protocol agreements. But, wealthy and politically connected California strawberry, fruit, and carrot farmers found their way around those restrictions and still were allowed to apply 7 million pounds in 2006 (the last year for which we have records). Methyl bromide causes birth defects, cardiac arrest, nervous system damage, and is responsible for many thousands of deaths since 1936.

The fifth most used chemical in California in 2006 was Telone II (1,3-Dichloropropene). Telone II is a cancer and birth defect-causing fumigant that has been very deadly and dangerous to farmers, farmworkers, school kids, and rural residents since the 1940s. When it first came out it was called 666. This is supposedly "The Mark of the Devil." Telone II has lived up to that name, killing and injuring untold thousands. Its California registration was due to be cancelled in 1995 because it was a cancer causing air pollutant. But, with the pending loss of methyl bromide, it was reregistered for limited use. They didn't apply real strict limitations, however, because California farmers used about 7 million pounds in 2006.

The sixth most used farm chemical in California was Chloropicrin. This chemical is tear gas, the highly effective anti-riot gas that is released in major demonstrations. One might ask "Why are we using tear gas on our food?" The answer is that it is a deadly biocide. It is usually combined with methyl bromide to provide a warning taste and smell (that methyl bromide lacks) and because it greatly increases the fumigation toxicity of both poisons. It causes several birth defects, causes severe respiratory damage, and is very toxic to fish. California farmers used 6.9 million pounds in 2006.

In 2004, California Strawberry growers used 184 pesticides. They applied an average of more than 335 pounds of pesticides per acre. Metam sodium, methyl bromide, chloropicrin and Telone II accounted for 74% (or 248 pounds) of the pesticides used on each acre of strawberries. Four of the world's most toxic chemicals, accounted for almost three-quarters of all pesticides used. Strawberry shortcake, anyone?

Data? What Data?: California is the only state that has collected pesticide use data in the U.S. (New York recently passed the same law). Unfortunately, for all the other states, we do not have good data. California began collecting use data from farmers and applicators in 1970. The USDA and most states only collect survey data, not actual usage amounts. Because California has real data, and because California provides half of the fresh produce in the country, their information is an invaluable guide to the level of poisonous exposure that U.S. farmers, farmworkers, food handlers, and customers have endured on farm products for almost forty years.

We analyzed the use of pesticides on crops from California's data set for the Sustainable Cotton Project and for *The War on Bugs* book. We found that factory farming has been very dependent on the worst poisons for all of the forty years that records have been kept. Although California has good data and toxicological analyses, it has not been aggressive in acting to cancel the registrations on even the chemicals it knows to be most poisonous, even those that cause multiple birth defects and cancer.

The USDA and each state should collect pesticide and fertilizer use data as California has for pesticides. Without real data, claims of increased or decreased use are groundless. Having the data will enable us to set real goals for chemical use reduction as European countries have. Then, and only then, will we be able to see if usage is declining or increasing and how many of the most toxic chemicals are used on our food and in our communities.

Besides collecting actual use data, we must evaluate all the farm and industrial chemicals as they are doing in the E.U. with REACH (Registration, Evaluation, And Authorization of Chemicals). Such data would greatly supplement the evaluations by Cal EPA and U.S.EPA, which are good, but significantly incomplete because they grandfathered in many chemicals that required no testing. REACH is currently evaluating even the grandfathered chemicals!

Even though our existing analyses are incomplete, the data from both CalEPA and U.S.EPA are sufficient to begin to phase out dozens of the most toxic pesticides. Many chemicals are so toxic that we need a goal of a 50% reduction every five years. We must begin these reductions because cancer and birth defect clusters are now common in most U.S. farm communities and people are being exposed to multiple pesticide residues on their fresh and processed food and on their clothing.

Confinement Animals/Excess Antibiotics and Hormones: I have pointed out in *The War on Bugs* and in other articles that our confinement animal operations (where most of our meat comes from) are a serious health and safety threat. And, as we have all come to realize, they are very poorly regulated. Overuse of hormones and antibiotics has left us with antibiotic resistant meat, large quantities of antibiotics in rivers and drinking water, and even antibiotic resistant pork farmers and consumers. Beef cows are often injected with hormones, milk cows with genetically modified growth hormones. The U.S. meat supply is so dangerously unhealthy that large amounts of it are regularly recalled (about 200,000,000 pounds of beef in 2008) and some of the more suspicious or contaminated meat has been allowed by the FDA to be irradiated since the 1990s. Nuked meat?

We raised 11 billion meat, milk, and egg-laying animals in the U.S. in 2008. By 2008, we produced nearly 69 million pigs, 95% in confinement. We raised 300 million commercial laying hens in battery cages. Ten billion meat chickens, and half a billion turkeys were confined in abusive close quarter conditions. About 33 million beef cows and 9.7 million dairy cows spent their dreary days in disgusting feedlots and dairy barns. These facilities and their meat products are rife with disease that the public is advised to combat by thorough cooking. In December, 2008 Consumer Reports found that 83% of the 525 meat chickens they studied had salmonella or campylobacter. With deadly diseases on all but 17 chickens out of 100, customers are asking: What about the salmonella on my drain board or my hands? No wonder there is so much food borne illness!

These enormous populations of animals also produce a lot of manure, and massive amounts of methane and nitrous oxide. The largest amount of nitrous oxide comes from fertilizer used on farmland that produces feed for confined animals. High methane emissions come from mountains of animal manure and digestive gasses, and a lesser though significant amount, from unsustainable grazing. Seventy to eighty percent of our farm production and acreage is used to produce the aforementioned 11 billion beef cows, pigs, poultry, milk cows, sheep, and goats. Fertilizer use in the U.S. is variable depending on the needs of the crop and the natural fertility of the land. Corn and cotton farmers, who grow the corn and cottonseed to feed these confined animals, use 200 to 300 pounds of nitrogen per acre and about 100 pounds of phosphorous. This is much more nitrogen and phosphorous than the crops can use in a single season, but the farmers are advised to use "enough" to get the highest possible yields. So, most of the nitrogen and phosphorous fertilizer that the plants don't need and can't use are flushed into rivers, lakes and the ocean.

I could continue further with this litany of unregulated farm problems, but these are the major issues. We are living in a very polluted and dangerous food world, partly because of the unregulated excesses of U.S. industrial farming. If we are going to bring down our high rates of obesity, diabetes, heart disease, cancer, and birth defects we have to change our food choices and how that food is raised. Besides creating profound health and safety problems, industrial farming is a huge unregulated contributor to global warming and an enormous user of energy. We must regulate and significantly reduce the U.S. farm use of fuels, pesticides, and fertilizer. These are not choices! These are necessities! If we are going to seriously tackle climate change and fix our health system, we have to change our form of agriculture.

We Can't Fix Factory Farming!: The Pew Charitable Trust and the Johns-Hopkins Bloomberg School of Public Health conducted a study in 2008 and determined that the U.S. factory farming system is dangerously out of control and that many practices, including animal confinement, and the prophylactic-use of antibiotics and hormones must be phased out. A second study, also in April of 2008, by the Union of Concerned Scientists concluded much the same. Both studies found that the current factory farming paradigms are simply not sustainable for the land, the drinking water, the confined animals, the rivers, and the oceans, and they are seriously damaging our public health. The Union of Concerned Scientists reminded us that we will be subsidizing these bad farming practices once again on April 15th when we pay our taxes. That is the second payment for "cheap food".

For more than one hundred years U.S. and European safe food activists' demanded real regulation of farm chemicals. But, it was always a pipe dream, since chemical firms, the universities and the government all alleged that the pesticides were safe and that farmers couldn't get good yields without chemicals. So, the regulators looked the other way. However, farmers around the world have demonstrated that they can produce as good or better yields of quality food and fiber without dangerous and damaging chemicals. Still, the regulators continue to look the other way and still refuse to stop the poisoning.

Salmonella contaminated pistachios, peanuts, tomatoes, melons, and jalapenos and the slaughtering of downer beef are glaring examples of sloppy farming and processing combined with regulatory failure. All of these regulatory failures and bad farming practices didn't just cause bankruptcy or a huge cut in 401-Ks, they sickened hundreds of millions and killed hundreds of thousands of people over the last thirty years!

Each day seems to bring more pesticide spills and injuries, more poisoned food, more contaminated drinking water, more dead zones and more residues on our food. Consequently, immediate regulation of and a rapid phase-out of the most toxic farm chemicals now seem like urgencies, instead of pipe dreams.

If We Can't Fix it, Let's Change it!: While U.S. factory farming can't be fixed, the good news is that changing U.S. agriculture it is not an unattainably complex goal. However, it does call for a paradigm shift. We must stop pretending that fossil based fertilizer and fuel is endless, sustainable, or environmentally justifiable. The Green Revolution is over! After one hundred years of use the jury is in. What looked in 1909 like a cheap and efficient fertilizer has polluted our drinking water, turned deadly to the oceans, is increasingly more expensive, and today is doing more harm than good. We must dramatically reduce the use of synthetic nitrogen fertilizer and began an immediate phase out.

In 1945, only five percent of the nitrogen used on U.S. farms was synthetic. Now, more than ninety-five percent is. Before the synthetic takeover, farmers grew fertilizer crops and applied small amounts of composted manure for fertility and tilth, to increase organic matter, and to feed the microorganisms. These techniques and more modern ones are used by both organic and non-organic farmers today and enable them to produce high yields of quality produce, meat, fiber, oilseeds, and grains. Farmers all over the world are getting higher yields of calories per acre on diversified organic farms than on monocultural chemical or GMO farms.

We can solve the dead zone problem by switching back from synthetic nitrogen and soluble phosphorous fertilizers to organic plant-based fertility. This is not rocket science and it is not a long shot with outmoded technology. It is, in fact, achievable within a few years. As a plus, fertilizer crops sequester carbon, which our currently barren soils in the fall and winter don't. We can eliminate the cancer and birth defect clusters and high pesticide residues on our favorite foods by using biological IPM strategies to control pests and diseases. Releasing beneficial insects, altering our growing practices, rotation of crops, soil balancing, and careful monitoring of pest damage are a few of the successful techniques that thousands of farmers are using to control pests and eliminate poisonous pesticides on their farms.

This is a challenging time for farmers, with many sorting out how can they produce their own energy on the farm as well as auditing and reducing their use. Most of us know that the cheap era of fossil fuel is over. With agriculture being responsible for such a large percentage of fossil fuel consumption, it is essential that resources be invested in alternative energy strategies by farmers, entrepreneurs, and by state and federal government agencies.

At this critical juncture, we should see these factory farm problems and their solutions as an opportunity. This is an opportunity for us to demand that Washington regulate our food supply. It is a chance to make real changes in our own diets by eating safe foods, supporting local organic farms, and frequenting farmers markets. Additionally, each of us can grow chemically free vegetables and fruits in our own yards, like the Obamas are doing at the White House.

It is also a time of opportunity to assist farmers and merchants in converting U.S. farming and the food system. To do this, we need much more government investment in the reinvigoration of our agricultural extension service. These new or retrained extension agents would help farmers make the transition to sustainable and organic agriculture (as some currently are). We also need access for young and not so young farmers to financial aid and government held farmland. Clearly, we also need lots more regulators. Only the government can address these issues. But, we must pressure the Obama run EPA, USDA, and FDA to address them as if they were urgent.

U.S. organic farmers developed a set of standards in the 1970s and 1980s to regulate farms and farmers with third party inspections. They did this to assure a suspicious public that the food they produced was really organic. The standards they enforce require crop rotation, an organic fertility and pest control program and prohibit the use of toxic fertilizers, chemical pesticides, hormones, antibiotics, genetic modification, sewage sludge, irradiation, and the feeding of animal protein to animals.

"Conventional" food in the U.S can be grown with all the farming practices outlawed in organic. Conventional is a semantic ploy to avoid calling the food "chemical," or "poisonous." Whatever you call it, it should be regulated and the most damaging practices should be made illegal.

Finally, we need to internationally harmonize our regulations, so that there is as much unanimity to the rules as possible and the enforcement is transparent. This is just as important in food as it is in finance. We are all too connected globally to pretend that we should not worry about another culture's food regulations or health concerns. Ideally, we should all embrace a more rigorous international REACH-like program that would protect farmers, farmworkers, processors and consumers.

Hopefully, the Obama administration attitude toward regulation will extend to U.S. agriculture. If it doesn't, we are in deep sh**! And, I'm not talking manure.

| "*Unfortunately, confining oneself to the scientific issues simply does not have the same impact in the public arena as holding up the specter of an imminent threat to our well-being.*"

Sloppy Analysis Shakes the Public's Faith in Science

Geoffrey Kabat

In the following viewpoint, Geoffrey Kabat examines the controversy over the herbicide glyphosate—the main ingredient in Monsanto's pesticide Roundup—and describes how the IARC (the International Agency for Research on Cancer) uses different criteria for declaring a substance to be a carcinogen than do most other agencies. This leads, argues Kabat, to confusion about the safety of the weed killer, undue alarm on the part of the public, and an undermining of the public's trust in science. Kabat is an epidemiologist and cancer researcher at Albert Einstein College of Medicine in New York.

As you read, consider the following questions:

1. How might conflicting interpretations of scientific data weaken the public's trust in science?

2. According to Kabat, the US Environment Protection Agency has been accused of both caving to the anti-pesticide movement and being overly influenced by companies such as Monsanto. How could the agency be influenced by both sides in this debate?

3. According to Robert Tarone, an expert quoted by Kabat, what mistakes did the IARC make in its evaluation of glyphosate?

On both sides of the Atlantic, a battle is raging between starkly opposed views of what science tells us about risks to our health emanating from our surroundings, including our food, water, and the wider environment.

This battle often pits advocates, nongovernmental organizations (NGOs), politicians, and partisan scientists, who have little ability or inclination to evaluate the evidence on its merits, against scientists and regulators who confine themselves to evaluating the evidence but are typically characterized as corrupt apologists for industry. Unfortunately, confining oneself to the scientific issues simply does not have the same impact in the public arena as holding up the specter of an imminent threat to our well-being, and the less sensationalist party in this lop-sided contest is often left to tear its hair out in frustration.

At the moment, a major focus in this battle is glyphosate, the most widely used herbicide (i.e., weed killer) in the United States. Glyphosate is the active ingredient in Monsanto's Roundup, and a number of major crops have been genetically engineered to be resistant to Roundup.

In response to a new report alleging a cancer risk from trace residues of glyphosate, which has sparked renewed pressure from anti-pesticide NGOs, this past June the European Union voted against re-registering glyphosate for agricultural use in Europe but agreed to an 18-month extension of the license. In the U.S. glyphosate is also at the center of a tangled regulatory battle.

Glyphosate and compounds containing the chemical, like Roundup, have been reviewed for health effects by a number of health agencies, including the European Food Safety Authority (EFSA), the Food and Agricultural Organization (FAO), Germany's Institute for Environment and Human Security (BfR), and the U.S. Environmental Protection Agency (EPA). These agencies have concluded that glyphosate is unlikely to pose a carcinogenic risk to humans.

However, in March 2015, the International Agency for Research on Cancer (IARC) classified glyphosate as a "probable carcinogen." IARC stated that its determination was based on "clear evidence of cancer in experimental animals, limited evidence for cancer for humans from real-world exposures, of exposed farmers, and also strong evidence that it can damage the genes and other toxicological studies."

A number of other recent determinations by IARC have perplexed both scientists and the public, most famously those pertaining to coffee, red meat, and cell phones. It has become clear that IARC takes a very different approach to assessing carcinogens than most other agencies. Rather than taking into account real-world exposure to an agent and what is known about its ability to cause cancer at various exposure levels—risk assessment—IARC's assessment takes into account the potential to cause cancer under theoretical conditions—hazard assessment. This approach is considered outmoded and unscientific by many scientists and regulatory agencies (accepted manuscript Boobis A, Cohen, S, Dellarco V, et al. "Classification schemes for carcinogenicity based on hazard-identification have become outmoded and serve neither science nor society," Regulatory Toxicology and Pharmacology, Oct. 2016).

Under IARC's "hazard assessment," weak and difficult-to-interpret findings can be given undue weight and can take precedence over other stronger types of evidence that do not point to a threat, such as that from epidemiologic studies in humans and whole animal studies.

Furthermore, for all IARC's claims of impartiality and rigor, in the case of glyphosate, its assessment is slipshod when it comes to critically examining what the key human and animal studies actually show.

Animal carcinogen testing involves taking a given strain of mice or rats and dividing them into different groups—usually receiving different doses of the substance under study as well as a control group that is given a placebo. The experiment runs for the lifespan of the test animals—1-2 years. As animals die, their tissues are examined by a pathologist. And at the end of the study, remaining animals are sacrificed, and their organs are examined. Benign and malignant changes in different organs are recorded.

What is crucial in evaluating the evidence from these studies is to look at all of the findings within each study for meaningful differences in the incidence of tumors between the exposed groups and the control group. A further expectation is that if tumors are caused by the agent, one should see a greater "tumor yield" at higher exposure levels, referred to as a "dose-response relationship." It is also important to compare what is found in male test animals with what is found in female animals. Finally, one needs to compare the results of different studies conducted in the same animal species to see whether there is consistency. Above all, one is looking for consistency and for a strong signal indicating that there is unambiguous evidence of the effect one is looking for.

In an article in the European Journal of Cancer Prevention, this past August the biostatistician Robert E. Tarone critically examined IARC's glyphosate assessment as well as the published articles cited by the Agency. Tarone spent most of his career at the National Cancer Institute (NCI) and then at the International Epidemiology Institute, which was founded by former NCI scientists. He was also a statistical editor for the Journal of the National Cancer Institute.

Tarone's exacting reexamination of the studies evaluated by IARC is a "lesson from the master" on how to review evidence rigorously and not be fooled by what one wants to find.

According to Tarone, probably the worst thing IARC did was to ignore mouse data that contradicted the story line supporting carcinogenicity.

In addition, IARC highlighted certain results from studies of Sprague-Dawley rats, as Tarone describes:

> The highlighting of selective marginally significant tumor increases in a single study without noting the complete absence of supporting evidence of tumor increases in two other studies using the same rat strain is a highly questionable scientific practice. Once again, a synthesis of the data from all three rat studies does not provide evidence in support of the hypothesis that glyphosate is associated with increased liver or thyroid C-cell tumor rates in Sprague–Dawley rats.

This is only one of the many examples in which the results highlighted by IARC do not withstand careful scrutiny.

Tarone concludes his discussion of animal studies as follows:

> Glyphosate would not have been classified by IARC as a probable human carcinogen except for the Working Group's conclusion that there was sufficient evidence of carcinogenicity in animals. When all relevant data from the rodent carcinogenicity studies of glyphosate relied upon by the Working Group are evaluated together, it is clear that the conclusion that there is sufficient evidence that glyphosate is an animal carcinogen is not supported empirically. Even a conclusion that there is limited evidence of animal carcinogenicity would be difficult to support on the basis of the rodent carcinogenicity assays of glyphosate reviewed by the IARC Working Group.

As far as the epidemiology is concerned, as mentioned earlier, there is a general consensus that the evidence that glyphosate is a human carcinogen is weak. IARC points to an association of glyphosate exposure with an increased risk of non-Hodgkin's lymphoma (NHL). But Tarone comments:

...the case made by IARC for a possible role of glyphosate in the etiology of NHL is quite weak. For example, the only significant finding reported for NHL and glyphosate in a US study (De Roos et al., 2003) is of questionable evidentiary weight. Glyphosate was one of 47 different pesticides evaluated for associations with NHL in this pooled analysis of case–control studies, and each pesticide was assessed using two different statistical methods. A significant association was reported between glyphosate and NHL for only one of the statistical methods applied.

In other words, IARC selected one result from among the many comparisons arising from applying two methods to the analysis of so many different pesticides. This selecting of a favored result exaggerates the significance of any risk due to glyphosate.

IARC's questionable finding that glyphosate is a "possible carcinogen" has been taken up by advocates and NGO's concerned about pesticides, including the National Resources Defense Council. A bizarre episode showcases the clash of different interest groups and interpretations regarding glyphosate. In October 2015, the EPA briefly released a report, labeled "final report," stating that glyphosate is not likely a carcinogen. But the agency quickly took the report down, saying it was a draft that was not meant to be published. The EPA's unexplained actions have provoked a firestorm of suspicion and charges that the agency is caving into anti-pesticide activists, as well as counter-charges that the agency is unduly influenced by commercial giants like Monsanto. A new meeting of the EPA Science Advisory Panel is scheduled for December. But changes to the make-up of the panel have provoked concern as to whether the Agency will give an unbiased assessment of the issue. A Congressional Committee is now investigating the EPA's process regarding glyphosate.

All of this points up just how politicized questions like the safety/carcinogenicity of glyphosate have become. The subtle and difficult-to-interpret results of animal experiments and studies of agricultural workers easily lend themselves to what different specialists with different points-of-view may wish to find in them. Meanwhile, the overlay of strong beliefs and ideological commitments threatens to obscure what the science has to say on a question of enormous economic importance.

What is at stake in this latest iteration of the clash over environmental threats is enormous. First, there is the possibility that a product that is cheap, safe, and effective will be restricted or banned, reducing crop yields and requiring the substitution of products about which less is known and which may pose a greater danger. Second, controversies like this cause unnecessary confusion and alarm in the public and divert attention from issues that really do matter. Third, by doing so, they add to the already considerable distrust of science.

*"As Cuba reoriented its agriculture
to depend less on imported chemical
inputs and imported equipment, food
production rebounded."*

An Agricultural Shift in Cuba Could Mean Ecological Disaster

Miguel Altieri

In the following viewpoint, Miguel Altieri focuses on the United States' recent normalization of relations with Cuba, which is expected to boost the Cuban economy and improve the lives of the Cuban people. However, Altieri argues, the move could have some unintended consequences. After the collapse of the Soviet Union, Cuba was deprived of an economic backer and moved toward a less-technology intensive, more ecologically sustainable agriculture. All that could change now that US agribusiness is back in the mix. Altieri is a professor of agroecology at the University of California, Berkeley.

As you read, consider the following questions:

1. Why did losing its partner, the Soviet Union, force changes in Cuba's agricultural methods?

2. According to Altieri, what role does urban agriculture play in Cuba's food system?

3. How does Altieri suggest that "economies of scale" might negatively affect Cuba's agricultural system?

P resident Obama's trip to Cuba this week accelerated the warming of U.S.-Cuban relations. Many people in both countries believe that normalizing relations will spur investment that can help Cuba develop its economy and improve life for its citizens.

But in agriculture, U.S. investment could cause harm instead.

For the past 35 years I have studied agroecology in most countries in Central and South America. Agroecology is an approach to farming that developed in the late 1970s in Latin America as a reaction against the top-down, technology-intensive and environmentally destructive strategy that characterizes modern industrial agriculture. It encourages local production by small-scale farmers, using sustainable strategies and combining Western knowledge with traditional expertise.

Cuba took this approach out of necessity when its economic partner, the Soviet bloc, dissolved in the early 1990s. As a result, Cuban farming has become a leading example of ecological agriculture.

But if relations with U.S. agribusiness companies are not managed carefully, Cuba could revert to an industrial approach that relies on mechanization, transgenic crops and agrochemicals, rolling back the revolutionary gains that its campesinos have achieved.

The shift to peasant agroecology

For several decades after Cuba's 1959 revolution, socialist bloc countries accounted for nearly all of its foreign trade.

The government devoted 30 percent of agricultural land to sugarcane for export, while importing 57 percent of Cuba's food supply. Farmers relied on tractors, massive amounts of pesticide and fertilizer inputs, all supplied by Soviet bloc countries. By the 1980s agricultural pests were increasing, soil quality was degrading and yields of some key crops like rice had begun to decline.

When Cuban trade with the Soviet bloc ended in the early 1990s, food production collapsed due to the loss of imported fertilizers, pesticides, tractors and petroleum. The situation was so bad that Cuba posted the worst growth in per capita food production in all of Latin America and the Caribbean.

But then farmers started adopting agroecological techniques, with support from Cuban scientists.

Thousands of oxen replaced tractors that could not function due to lack of petroleum and spare parts. Farmers substituted green manures for chemical fertilizers and artisanally produced biopesticides for insecticides. At the same time, Cuban policymakers adopted a range of agrarian reform and decentralization policies that encouraged forms of production where groups of farmers grow and market their produce collectively.

As Cuba reoriented its agriculture to depend less on imported chemical inputs and imported equipment, food production rebounded. From 1996 though 2005, per capita food production in Cuba increased by 4.2 percent yearly during a period when production was stagnant across Latin America and the Caribbean.

In the mid-2000s, the Ministry of Agriculture dismantled all "inefficient state companies" and government-owned farms, endorsed the creation of 2,600 new small urban and suburban farms, and allowed farming on some three million hectares of unused state lands.

Urban gardens, which first sprang up during the economic crisis of the early 1990s, have developed into an important food source.

Today Cuba has 383,000 urban farms, covering 50,000 hectares of otherwise unused land and producing more than 1.5 million tons of vegetables. The most productive urban farms yield up to

20 kg of food per square meter, the highest rate in the world, using no synthetic chemicals. Urban farms supply 50 to 70 percent or more of all the fresh vegetables consumed in cities such as Havana and Villa Clara.

The risks of opening up

Now Cuba's agriculture system is under increasing pressure to deliver harvests for export and for Cuba's burgeoning tourist markets. Part of the production is shifting away from feeding local and regional markets, and increasingly focusing on feeding tourists and producing organic tropical products for export.

President Obama hopes to open the door for U.S. businesses to sell goods to Cuba. In Havana last Monday during Obama's visit, U.S. Agriculture Secretary Tom Vilsack signed an agreement with his Cuban counterpart, Agriculture Minister Gustavo Rodriguez Rollero, to promote sharing of ideas and research.

"U.S. producers are eager to help meet Cuba's need for healthy, safe, nutritious food," Vilsack said. The U.S. Agriculture Coalition for Cuba, which was launched in 2014 to lobby for an end to the U.S.-Cuba trade embargo, includes more than 100 agricultural companies and trade groups. Analysts estimate that U.S. agricultural exports to Cuba could reach US$1.2 billion if remaining regulations are relaxed and trade barriers are lifted, a market that U.S. agribusiness wants to capture.

When agribusinesses invest in developing countries, they seek economies of scale. This encourages concentration of land in the hands of a few corporations and standardization of small-scale production systems. In turn, these changes force small farmers off of their lands and lead to the abandonment of local crops and traditional farming ways. The expansion of transgenic crops and agrofuels in Brazil, Paraguay and Bolivia since the 1990s are examples of this process.

If U.S. industrial agriculture expands into Cuba, there is a risk that it could destroy the complex social network of agroecological small farms that more than 300,000 campesinos have built up over the past several decades through farmer-to-farmer horizontal exchanges of knowledge.

This would reduce the diversity of crops that Cuba produces and harm local economies and food security. If large businesses displace small-scale farmers, agriculture will move toward export crops, increasing the ranks of unemployed. There is nothing wrong with small farmers capturing a share of export markets, as long as it does not mean neglecting their roles as local food producers. The Cuban government thus will have to protect campesinos by not importing food products that peasants produce.

Cuba still imports some of its food, including U.S. products such as poultry and soybean meal. Since agricultural sales to Cuba were legalized in 2000, U.S. agricultural exports have totaled about $5 billion. However, yearly sales have fallen from a high of $658 million in 2008 to $300 million in 2014.

U.S. companies would like to regain some of the market share that they have lost to the European Union and Brazil.

There is broad debate over how heavily Cuba relies on imports to feed its population: the U.S. Department of Agriculture estimates that imports make up 60 to 80 percent of Cubans' caloric intake, but other assessments are much lower.

In fact, Cuba has the potential to produce enough food with agroecological methods to feed its 11 million inhabitants. Cuba has about six million hectares of fairly level land and another million gently sloping hectares that can be used for cropping. More than half of this land remains uncultivated, and the productivity of both land and labor, as well as the efficiency of resource use, in the rest of this farm area are still low.

We have calculated that if all peasant farms and cooperatives adopted diversified agroecological designs, Cuba would be able to produce enough to feed its population, supply food to the tourist industry and even export some food to help generate foreign currency.

President Raul Castro has stated that while opening relations with the U.S. has some benefits,

We will not renounce our ideals of independence and social justice, or surrender even a single one of our principles, or concede a millimeter in the defense of our national sovereignty. We have won this sovereign right with great sacrifices and at the cost of great risks.

Cuba's small farmers control only 25 percent of the nation's agricultural land but produce over 65 percent of the country's food, contributing significantly to the island's sovereignty. Their agroecological achievements represent a true legacy of Cuba's revolution.

Periodical and Internet Sources Bibliography

The following articles have been selected to supplement the diverse views presented in this chapter.

Debbie Barker and Michael Pollan, "A Secret Weapon to Fight Climate Change: Dirt," *Washington Post*, December 15, 2015.

Matthew Bershadker, "Make 'Organic' Mean Something," *Huffington Post* blog, June 23, 2016. http://www.huffingtonpost.com/matt -bershadker/making-organic-mean-somet_b_10636184.html.

David Biello, "Why Don't Farmers Believe in Climate Change, and Does It Really Matter Whether They Do?" *Slate*, July 16, 2013. http://www.slate.com/articles/technology future_ tense2013/07farmers_don_t_believe_in_climate_change_but_ maybe_that_s_ok.html.

David Maxwell Braun, "Factory Farming Is Not the Best We Have to Offer," *National Geographic*, October 13, 2011. http://voices .nationalgeographic.com/2011/10/13/factory-farming-is-not-the -best-we-have-to-offer.

Louise O. Fresco, "Splat Goes the Theory," *Aeon*, November 10, 2015.

Christina Gillham, "Are Locavores Really Green?" *Newsweek.com*, September 22, 2009. http://www.newsweek.com/environment -are-locavores-really-green-79401.

Phil Limpet, "Why Factory Farming Isn't What You Think," Forbes.com, June 15, 2015. http://www.forbes.com/sites /phillempert/2015/06/15/why-factory-farming-isnt-what-you -think/#48a965ba59d0.

Jayson Lusk, "Why Industrial Farms Are Good for the Environment," *New York Times*, September 23, 2016. http://www.nytimes .com/2016/09/25/opinion/sunday/why-industrial-farms-are -good-for-the-environment.html?_r=0.

Bradford Plumer, "The New Republic: The Environment Paradox," National Public Radio website, September 2, 2010. http://www .npr.org/templates/story/story.php?storyId=129598408.

Bryan Walsh, "The Triple Whopper Environmental Impact of Global Meat Production," *Time*, December 16, 2013. http://science.time .com/2013/12/16/the-triple-whopper-environmental-impact-of -global-meat-production.

CHAPTER 3

Is Corporate Farming Economically Sustainable?

Chapter Preface

E ven among those who have serious concerns about the safety of large-scale corporate, industrial farming, there is debate about how economically sustainable is the alternative. The large amounts of chemical inputs used by large-scale agriculture (pesticides and fertilizers, for example) can increase the price of crops, while organic methods rely on more cost-efficient methods such as composting, crop rotation, and companion planting to achieve the same ends. However, small-scale and organic farming tends to be much more labor-intensive, perhaps offsetting at least some of the cost savings. For many small farmers, the math just doesn't add up. They can grow enough food, but making a profit from it is a serious challenge. Small farmers may be able to feed the world, but can they feed (and clothe and house) their families while doing so?

On the other hand, according to recent data from the United States Department of Agriculture, the income of the average farm family is considerably higher than that of a non-farm family. However, most farmers depend on supplemental off-farm income, investments, and savings to tide them over in bad years.

In addition, questions about the most efficient way of producing crops, how best to get foods from farm to market, and how to overcome the challenges of getting food from growing regions to regions where food is desperately needed all complicate the economics of food production. When considering the cost of a product, whether it be food or any other commodity, one must take into account hidden costs. In agriculture, these are often the costs to the environment or human health. Factoring this in changes the equation but does not necessarily produce clear answers.

In this chapter, we will hear from a small, independent farmer who makes a comfortable living at this trade—as his family has done for generations. And he has suggestions about how others might do so as well. But we'll also meet a young, independent farmer who is struggling to stay afloat—unable to pay her expenses without the help of non-farm income, and living precariously close to poverty. Yet another family farmer explains why small farmers feel so much pressure to get bigger.

> "Our food system should be a
> community-based system that
> revolves around small, polycultural
> farms that practice sustainable
> agriculture, preserve regional
> biodiversity and help build
> local economies."

Local Food Economies Can Thrive

Olga Bonfiglio

In the following viewpoint, Olga Bonfiglio questions the economic sustainability of small farms from the perspective of one US state— Michigan. According to the author, there is a great deal of opportunity for local food economies to thrive in Michigan, and she details many interesting programs and initiatives for locally grown and organic food. The state, however, is still entrenched in the industrial food system. This article was written in 2009 and cites data from the previous year; however it provides an interesting and helpful snapshot of the influence of such things as weather and gas prices on food prices, and the impact of local initiatives. Bonfiglio is a writer and professor at Kalamazoo College in Kalamazoo, Michigan.

"Opportunity Knocks When It Comes to a Local Food Economy," by Olga Bonfiglio, Common Dreams, February 6, 2009. http://www.commondreams.org/views/2009/02/06/ opportunity-knocks-when-it-comes-local-food-economy. Licensed under CC BY-SA 3.0.

As you read, consider the following questions:

1. What is one problem Bonfiglio sees with the economics of local organic food?
2. How, according to this article, are colleges and universities helping make local, organic food economically viable?
3. Where does Bonfiglio say that most people in Michigan get their food?

Community-based agriculture has the potential for creating jobs, developing small business entrepreneurships and keeping precious dollars in the community.

"As manufacturing jobs decrease, food jobs are increasing," said Dr. Kami Pothukuchi, associate professor of urban planning at Wayne State University in Detroit.

This is especially good news for a state like Michigan whose economic engine has been dependent on the declining automobile industry.

Out of a total GDP of $381 billion, agriculture is the state's second largest industry pulling in $63.7 billion annually compared to $68.4 billion from manufacturing, according to the Michigan Department of Agriculture (MDA) and the U.S. Bureau of Labor Statistics.

However, the present "industrialized food system" is made up of a handful of "mega-corporations" that control food production, processing, distribution and preparation, said Pothukuchi. Change to a community-based system is difficult because these corporations have a lot at stake in keeping the current system.

The U.S. industrialized food system was designed in the 1950s to increase production in order to provide the nation with cheap and plentiful food that was easily accessible. As a result, the United States became a top food producer in the world.

A variety of food-related jobs in processing, marketing and distribution also emerged even though the number of farmers declined. The U.S. Department of Agriculture Census (USDA) reported that farms increased in size averaging 155 acres in 1935, a peak year when the country had 6.8 million farms, compared to 2002 when farms averaged 441 acres and numbered 2.1 million farms.

It is important to remember that the industrialized food system was developed at a time when most American businesses were creating systems for mass production and economies of scale. Because volume is critical to the profitability of this system, farming methods developed to support a large-scale, energy-intensive monoculture that uses huge amounts of water and chemicals for herbicides, insecticides, and fertilizers. Tons of animal waste products also accumulate and pollute land, water and air because factory farming methods keep animals indoors and free of disease instead of allowing them to graze in pastures.

Actually, the cost of the industrialized food system outweighs its benefits. For example, most food in the industrialized system ends up in supermarkets after traveling an average 1,300 miles to get there. Fruits and vegetables may spend seven to fourteen days in transit. So freshness and taste are sacrificed for the products' ability to travel.

Transporting products has been possible through cheap fuel. However, when oil reached over $100 a barrel last spring, the expense incurred over such long distances proved problematic. For example, world food prices averaged an increase of 43 percent over the past year, which inadvertently created a global food crisis that is causing political and economical instability and social unrest in both poor and developed nations.

Unseasonable droughts in grain-producing nations also affects high food prices just as falling stockpiles, the increased use of biofuels in developed countries and increasing demands for meat products in Asia's middle class, according the BBC (May 2008).

The Consumer Price Index estimates that U.S. retail food prices increased in 2007 by only 4 percent, but this is the largest spike in 17 years-with more expected to come.

Industrial farming practices were developed when world population was only 2 billion. While these practices increased the carrying capacity of the earth then, they are slowly destroying the earth's long-term carrying capacity for today's population, which is 6.7 billion and climbing.

Over the past two decades as the industrialized food system has expanded to the global level, concerns over food safety have emerged, like the recent tainted food imports from China.

The industrialized food system has had a detrimental effect on the local economy, said Pothukuchi. Our food system should be a community-based system that revolves around small, polycultural farms that practice sustainable agriculture, preserve regional biodiversity and help build local economies. This is already being done in many ways.

First, local food networks like community gardens, food co-ops, Community-Supported Agriculture (CSA), farmers' markets, and seed savers groups keep money in the community.

Second, as more people prefer organic food products, organic farming represents a profitable alternative for local economic growth and sustainable agriculture since organic farmers tend to sell to local markets (within 150 miles). More acreage is being dedicated to organic farming. From 1997 to 2005, the number of U.S. certified organic acres grew by 63 percent, while Michigan certified organic farmland increased by 166 percent.

In actuality, the number of industrialized farms converting to organic farming methods remains steady, but small. Michigan's 45,500 certified organic acres comprise only 0.4 percent of the state's total farmland and 1 percent of the total 4,000,000 certified organic acres in the country according to the Michigan Organic Farm and Food Alliance (MOFFA). But the potential for growth is there, especially when organic food processors/handlers are figured into the economic mix. The USDA reports that there were over 3,000 organic-certified facilities nationwide in 2004, with 41 percent of those located on the Pacific Coast and almost 800 in California alone.

Local organic food is admittedly more expensive than food from large, industrialized farms, however, organic advocates claim that prices in the industrialized food system are cheap because their true cost omits governmental price supports, direct payments or tax breaks and road infrastructure.

Third, colleges and universities across the country are looking for ways to support sustainable agriculture. One way they are doing it is by supplying their cafeterias with food grown by local farmers. These institutions teach students how to grow backyard and community gardens as well as food-related careers like urban farming. Pothukuchi started an urban gardening program at Wayne State, which is distinguished as the largest inner-city campus with a comprehensive food systems program that is not run by an agriculture school.

Some areas of the state are actively recruiting youth for community-based farming careers through hands-on learning situations. The 4-H Entrepreneurs Club in Kalkaska County has youth pick and buy produce at area farms in order to sell it at five different farmers markets. There are similar programs in Detroit and Monroe County.

Fourth, regions like Grand Traverse in the northwestern lower peninsula, are rebuilding their local economies through agriculture by forming partnerships among businesspeople, economic developers, schools, grocers, restaurateurs and food retailers, reported the Great Lakes Bulletin News Service. As these partnerships work to bring more food-related jobs to the area, they not only support local farmers but they also protect precious income-producing farmlands from being overtaken by urban sprawl.

The Michigan Land Use Institute (MLUI) speculates that the Grand Traverse region could stimulate more job growth and entrepreneurship by supporting its 2,229 farms through cooperative efforts like the Food and Farm Network. Moreover, a 2006 MLUI study found that farms could generate 1,889 new jobs across the state and $187 million in new personal income by selling more fresh produce locally.

Fifth, state programs can provide yet another opportunity for local economic development, like the MDA's Agricultural Innovation Program. This competitive grant seeks to establish, retain, expand, attract or develop value-added processing and production operations in Michigan through innovative financing assistance to processors, agribusinesses, producers, local units of government and legislatively-authorized commodity boards in Michigan.

All these efforts for change, however, have barely dented the deeply-entrenched industrialized food system. Michigan residents, for example, spend $26 billion on food with only 10 percent from the state's farmers, according to a 2001 MLUI study.

"Michigan has the second most diverse agriculture in the United States [with 150 crops]," said Pothukuchi. "We could add another $2.6 billion to the state's economy if we increased production of local food by another 10 percent."

> *"I see a lot of talk about big ag and small local and very few people seem to really understand what's going on. So let's talk about why small farms are being replaced by larger farms."*

Farms Get Big Out of Economic Necessity

Carrie Mess

In the following viewpoint, Carrie Mess uses personal experience to weigh in on family farming. While her family farm is considered about average size for her area, Mess dispels common notions about family farming and explains why many family farms are forced to get bigger. According to Mess, it is not necessarily big agriculture eating up all the farmland but both economic and lifestyle decisions of individual farmers that drive them to scale up their operations. Mess is a blogger and dairy farmer in Wisconsin.

As you read, consider the following questions:

1. What is one reason Mess says farmers often have to expand their operations?
2. How might having to borrow money from a bank to repair barns or buy livestock force a farm to increase production?
3. What lifestyle concerns does Mess say famers face that people in other occupations do not?

"5 Reasons Farms Are Getting Bigger," dairycarrie, May 27, 2014. Reprinted by permission.

There seems to be a lot of talk these days about large farms squeezing out the small farms. I see small farmers complaining about big farmers gobbling up land. I see people in the city lamenting the passing of the picturesque red barn farms. I see a lot of talk about big ag and small local and very few people seem to really understand what's going on. So let's talk about why small farms are being replaced by larger farms.

Hubs and I farm in a partnership with his parents. We milk around 100 cows and grow crops on around 300 acres. In Wisconsin, where we live, the average dairy farm is 100 cows. So we are your average sized farm for our area. We have a couple of part time employees that milk a few milkings a week, we have a full time employee that helps us get everything done. Hubs and both of his parents derive their income solely from the farm. I work on the farm as well as off the farm and do not take pay from the farm. Right now the amount of income that our cows produce can sustain the farm and the people who draw a paycheck from it. However, we are far from living a lavish lifestyle. There aren't piles of money lying around that I have found. Most people would classify us as a "small farm."

As a small farmer I don't understand when other farmers complain about "big" farms pushing them out. I don't see it. I hear people say that they could have bought some land but some "big farmer" came in and paid more than they could offer. This seems a lot like someone saying that they didn't buy a car because someone else offered more than they were willing to pay, and blaming that person for it.

5 Reasons why farms are getting bigger

Farms have to get bigger to generate enough income to support more family members when kids decide to join the family business. If a farm only generates enough profit for 1 household you can't expect it to suddenly make enough profit for 2 households without some major changes. Despite what you may have seen in headlines around the internet, around 98% of all US farms are family owned.

COMMUNITY SUPPORTED AGRICULTURE CAN IMPROVE LOCAL COMMUNITIES

Despite their typically small size and sparse distribution, farms that sell their products locally may boost economic growth in their communities in some regions of the U.S., according to a team of economists. The team's findings, which appear in the February 2014 issue of Economic Development Quarterly, shed new light on the role that local food sales play in economies ...by establishing that direct sales have a positive effect on total agricultural sales, which in turn have an effect on income growth, this study demonstrates that direct sales do indeed expand local economies at least in the Northeast U.S. ...

"When we set out to measure the economic impact of local food sales, we frankly didn't expect to find one," said Stephen Goetz, professor of agricultural and regional economics at Penn State's College of Agricultural Sciences. He explained that economists are generally skeptical that local sales can have impacts because such sales tend to recirculate money within a community rather than inject new money. "Injection of new money—money from outside of the community—is what many economic development practitioners think of as the fuel for economic growth. But to me, these findings provide quite robust evidence that even direct sales do have an effect on growth, in the Northeast U.S."

"Local Foods Offer Tangible Economic Benefits in Some Regions," by Kristen Devlin, Pennsylvania State University, February 3, 2014.

Do you like spending time with your friends? How about having weekends off? What about sleeping in or going on vacation? On a small farm you don't get those things easily if at all. You are tied to the farm, even more so when you have livestock. Cows, chickens and pigs aren't like a house cat, you can't just fill up their food bowl and tell them you'll see them tomorrow. Without employees to care for the animals, your free time is very limited. In order to afford employees, you have to generate enough profit to pay them.

Farms are getting bigger because there are fewer people willing to do the work. The average age of farmers in the US is 55 years old. I know many more farmers whose children live in the city and don't have any plans to return to the farm than farmers who are handing off their farms to the next generation. Farming is hard work and you don't make much money. It's not surprising that many people choose to leave the farm. Fewer people willing to do the work means that those who do want to do the work get bigger.

Farming is expensive. In our area good cropland sells for $8-10,000 an acre. Tractors and equipment can cost BIG money. Want to have livestock? Then you have buildings, they cost money too. Oh, and cows and pigs don't grow on trees, you have to buy them as well. It is not easy for someone to get into farming. This keeps a lot of people from coming into farming and that keeps small farms from starting or staying in business. As you grow your farm, the bank is more likely to loan you money to improve your facilities for your animals or equipment. They won't give you a million dollar loan to build a barn for 22 cows because 22 cows would never be able to generate enough income to pay the bank back. Want a shop to work on your tractor? You better be able to show the bank that you can make the loan payments.

Profit margins in farming aren't awesome. Like any business we have to pay close attention to the dollars coming in and going out. As farms grow they buy larger amounts of needed items like seed, vaccinations, feed ingredients, fuel, etc. As anybody with a Costco or Sam's membership knows buying in bulk can save you loads of money. I doubt that any farmer is doubling the size of their farm to save $.10 on a gallon of motor oil but knowing that there are ways to improve your profit margin as your farm grows is an incentive to do so.

Hubs and I hope to keep our farm about the same size it is now. We both agree that we would rather manage our cows and not manage people. We know that we are hands on people and we want to be the ones to do the hands on work with our crops and cows. That being said, we also know that we are going to need to figure out ways to make out farm more profitable so that we can stay the size we are. For us that means looking at ways to get more money for our milk, like marketing cheese made with milk from our cows. We are also looking at ways to cut our labor costs, like installing milking robots when our current parlor needs to be replaced, saving us money on hiring part time employees. We know we have to get creative to stay the size that we are in the future and we don't hold anything against those who decide to grow. Small or large, it's going to take all of us to feed the world.

> *"All government really has to do is provide a level playing field where small intensive farming can compete fairly with large, heavily-subsidized, industrial farming and then stand back."*

Small Farming Could Create Jobs, If Big Industry Would Step Back and Let Them

Gene Logsdon

In the following viewpoint from his blog the Contrary Farmer, Gene Logsdon draws on his own experience having grown up on a family farm and continued that tradition to argue that small family farms are economically efficient. Such farms could create many jobs if the government would level the playing field so that small farmers could compete fairly with large industrial operations, he says. Logsdon, who was known by the nickname "the Contrary Farmer" because of his outspoken criticism of modern farming, expresses his views in a straightforward, friendly, and often humorous way. Logsdon was a writer, cultural and economic critic, and farmer who used traditional farming methods. He died in May 2016.

"Small Farms Create More Jobs," by Gene Logsdon, September 14, 2011. Reprinted by permission.

As you read, consider the following questions:

1. Why does Logsdon say that we have created an economy that can't afford to pay people to do the work?

2. What is the benefit of family farms for young people, according to Logsdon?

3. Why, according to Logsdon, does government not make policy that would create jobs by supporting small farms?

All the talk about creating jobs strikes me as another example of how so many of us sneakily drink one way and piously vote another. Oh how we voice our concern, how much we pretend to support more jobs but we go right on conducting real business on the basis of replacing human workers with machines whenever possible. All the ways being proposed to increase jobs right now are the same old methods that do not face the real cause of the dilemma. The awful truth is that we have created an economy that can't afford people to do the work and so every year there are fewer meaningful jobs and more pretend jobs. Pretend jobs require pretend money. We are capitalizing costs on money interest not on human interest.

No where is this truer than in farming. We boast about how many people one farmer feeds—155 is the latest number I think—as if that kind of efficiency is a sign of progress. I don't hear a single business person or government official pointing out that if the whole economy of the common good is considered, one farmer feeding 155 people is not a sign of true profitability but of gross and unsustainable inefficiency. So gross in fact that while the 155 are getting fed, others are going hungry.

It is fairly easy, I think, to demonstrate the inefficiency of one person feeding a hundred and fifty-five especially when some of the hundred and fifty-five are having a hard time earning enough to buy their food. You can quibble with me on exact numbers, but modern machinery and technology makes it possible for one farmer to grow about 5000 acres of corn with one employee. One almost humorous example of this is how tractors can now guide themselves across unbroken acres of land without human help although a driver is still necessary to turn the tractor at the end of the field. That will soon not be necessary either, I'm told, and so one more "problem" will be avoided: how to stay awake in the tractor. One tractor driver advocates a stack of magazines, not necessarily the kind you leave out on your coffee table.

You can say that manufacturing high tech farm machinery creates jobs, but more and more of the manufacturing is also being done by robotic technology. The robots can even manufacture themselves now with less and less human input.

Let us say that the 5000 acre corn farmer must spend $800 an acre to put that crop out. Again you can quibble over the exact numbers but he has about four million dollars tied up in the crop before he harvests one ear of corn. The cost could be more or less than that depending on what he paid for fertilizer or what he pays his employee or what he pays in rent or interest on investment. But four million is close enough and by the time that corn is dried, stored and transported half way across the country to feed factory hogs and chickens, who knows how much more cost is involved including the attendant pollution and road degradation that the animal factories far out in the country must deal with. And industrial farmers are being subsidized heftily. If the corn is used to make ethanol, which is subsidized to high heaven too, and then fed to cars while poor people go hungry, the true cost to society becomes incalculable.

On the other hand, it is still quite possible for a small traditional farmer to make a living on 300 acres of land, of which about 30 acres will go to corn to feed livestock. A generation or two ago, corn could be planted with rather primitive machinery and harvested mostly by hand. My father did it with family help and we certainly didn't think we were slaves. Corn on such farms is fed right there to make milk, meat, and eggs. No transportation costs except from the back forty to the barn are involved. Or let the pigs "hog off" the corn for zero harvest and transportation costs.

You get the point even if my figures aren't perfectly accurate. The 5000 acres of industrial corn, which is employing two people, could be providing jobs and homes for about 17 family farmers and their wives and children. Run all the figures and all the farmland out to a logical mathematical conclusion and the number of new jobs created by restructuring agriculture is unbelievably awesome. There are about 90 million acres in corn this year. That would make 300,000 family farms of 300 acres each. That means 600,000 parents would be fully employed and let us say two teenagers who are trying desperately right now to find part time jobs,— a total of 1,200,000 new jobs. If we take into account industrial soybean, wheat, and cotton acreages as well and divide all that land into 300 acre family farms, the number of new jobs created rockets to somewhere in the three to five million range.

If you say that a family can't make a living on 300 acres, I beg to differ. I have lots of friends who do it. Steve and Pat Gamby do it with an organic dairy farm and they are far from Amish. Bob Kidwell does it on 120 acres farming with horses and he's not Amish either. Andy Reinhart and Jan Dawson do it on about two acres with organic vegetables, fruit and flowers.

Part of the reason, maybe most of the reason, why farmers' markets and local foods are enjoying such a renaissance is because they are creating new jobs the right way. All government really has to do is provide a level playing field where small intensive farming can compete fairly with large, heavily-subsidized, industrial farming and then stand back. A revolution will take place in new job creation and it will be in the right direction: more good food and a more stable society at a lesser overall cost. Right now, big business and big government like to talk earnestly about more jobs, but oh my, not in areas where new jobs might threaten big industry.

> *"According to USDA data from 2012, intermediate-size farms like mine, which gross more than $10,000 but less than $250,000, obtain only 10 percent of their household income from the farm, and 90 percent from an off-farm source."*

Family Farming Can't Support a Family

Jaclyn Moyer

So far in this text, we've heard from at least one small farmer who says that people can and are making a living as small farmers. In the following viewpoint, Jaclyn Moyer argues that it is virtually impossible for small farmers to make an adequate living at their trade. She cites data from the United States Department of Agriculture as well as drawing on her own experience and that of fellow farmers, to make the case that small farming is economically unsustainable. Moyer is a farmer who grows organic vegetables in northern California.

"What Nobody Told Me About Small Farming: I Can't Make A Living," by Jaclyn Moyer, Associated Press, February 10, 2015. This article first appeared in Salon.com at http://www.Salon.com. An online version remains in the Salon archives. Reprinted with permission.

As you read, consider the following questions:

1. Does Moyer explain why it is so difficult for small farmers to earn a living?
2. What criteria did the author set for making a living as a farmer?
3. Based on things you've read elsewhere in this book, do you have any ideas about why Moyer is having more trouble than, say, Logsdon (in the previous viewpoint) making a living at farming?

On the radio this morning I heard a story about the growing number of young people choosing to become farmers. The farmers in the story sounded a lot like me—in their late 20s to mid-30s, committed to organic practices, holding college degrees, and from middle-class non-farming backgrounds. Some raise animals or tend orchards. Others, like me, grow vegetables. The farmers' days sounded long but fulfilling, drenched in sun and dirt. The story was uplifting, a nice antidote to the constant reports of industrial ag gone wrong, of pink slime and herbicide-resistant super-weeds.

What the reporter didn't ask the young farmers was: *Do you make a living? Can you afford rent, healthcare? Can you pay your labor a living wage?* If the reporter had asked me these questions, I would have said no.

My farm is located in the foothills of Northern California, 40 miles east of Sacramento on 10 acres my partner, Ryan, and I lease from a land trust. In the heat of summer, my fields cover the bronzed landscape like a green quilt spread over sand. Ten acres of certified organic vegetables trace the contours of a small valley floor. Tomatoes glow crimson. Flowers bloom: zinnias, lavender, daisies. Watermelons grow fat, littering the ground like beach balls.

A businessman once advised me never to admit my business was struggling. *No one wants to climb aboard a sinking ship, know what I mean?* he'd said. At the time, I agreed. I believed if a business was failing it was because the entrepreneur was not skilled enough, not savvy enough, not hardworking enough. If my farm didn't turn enough profit, it was my own fault.

Whenever a customer asked how things were going, I replied, *Great*. I thought about the sinking ship, and never said, *Well, we're making ends meet, but we work 12 hour days, 6 days a week, and pay ourselves only what we need to cover food and household expenses: $100 per week*. I didn't tell anyone how, over the course of the last three years since Ryan and I had started our farm, I'd drained most of my savings. I didn't admit that the only thing keeping the farm afloat was income Ryan and I earned through other means—Ryan working as a carpenter and I as a baker. I didn't say that despite the improvements we made to the land—the hundreds of yards of compost we spread, the thousand dollars we spent annually on cover crop seed to increase soil fertility, every weed pulled—we gained no equity because we didn't own the land. I didn't say I felt like I was trying to fill a bathtub when the drain was open.

One afternoon, a fellow farmer came over for a visit. He asked how we were doing, and this time I told the truth. The farmer told me he'd been farming for nearly a decade and last year he made the most profit yet: $4,000. I spewed out a slurry of concerns, told the farmer how I'd done the numbers every way and the future wasn't looking much more profitable. The farmer just nodded, as if I was telling him what I'd eaten for breakfast that morning and not revealing the shameful secret of my failing business. The more we talked the more I began to wonder about other farmers I knew.

I wondered how many small farmers actually made a living. Before I set out trying to answer this question, I had to define what constitutes "a living." I decided making a living meant three things: 1) The farmer had to pay herself a weekly wage that equaled what a person working full-time would make on minimum wage, which in my town would be $360 per week. 2) The farmer had to abide by labor laws, meaning no unpaid workers or interns doing essential farm tasks. 3) The farmer had to earn her income from farming, which meant nonprofit farms that survived on grants and donations didn't count; neither did farms that sustained themselves on outside income sources.

I talked to all the farmers I knew, considered farms I or my partner had worked at in the past, farms I'd visited, friends' farms. Most farmers I talked to worked outside jobs to keep their farms above water, others skirted by on an income they calculated to be $4 per hour, and most depended on interns, volunteers or WWOOFers for labor. I did not encounter a single farmer who met my requirements.

Then I looked into national statistics. According to USDA data from 2012, intermediate-size farms like mine, which gross more than $10,000 but less than $250,000, obtain only 10 percent of their household income from the farm, and 90 percent from an off-farm source. Smaller farms actually lost money farming and earned 109 percent of their household income from off-farm sources. Only the largest farms, which represent just 10 percent of farming households in the country and most of which received large government subsidies, earned the majority of their income from farm sources. So, 90 percent of farmers in this country rely on an outside job, or a spouse's outside job, or some independent form of wealth, for their primary income.

One day late into my second season owning the farm, a customer walked in while I stood behind the counter spraying down bins of muddy carrots. The man asked how things were going. *Financially, I mean.* He held a head of lettuce in the crook of his arm, a bundle of pink radishes dangled from his hand.

I looked at the man and instead of replying with my usual "great," I said, *We're getting by.* He nodded, *Well, you may not be making lots of money, but you're rich in other ways.* I opened my mouth to reply, but the man had already turned away and was gazing dreamy-eyed out at my fields, each row buttered in late-afternoon sun. I turned back to the heap of carrots, not sure what I would have said anyway.

I wanted to ask the man which "other ways" did he mean, exactly. But I knew what he meant. I heard this kind of thing all the time: *You must love what you do, or not much profit in farming, but what a great lifestyle, or, well, you're not in it for the money, right?* Customers repeated these aphorisms warmly in an attempt to offer me some consolation or encouragement. But watching this man gaze out at my fields, I couldn't help wondering if it was the customer who was the one being consoled.

Surely many farmers enjoy what they do, as I often find pleasure in my daily tasks, but ultimately farming is work, an occupation, a means of making a living that must fulfill the basic function of a job: to provide an income. Does the notion that farming is lovable work excuse the fact that the entire industry relies on underpaid labor? Does it somehow make it OK that in 2014 it's forecast to be $-1,682$? I had to wonder if this notion works only to assuage a collective discomfort provoked by an unsettling fact, a fact that should enrage us, that should disgrace us as a society: the fact that the much celebrated American small farmer can't even make a living.

A few weeks later I gave a presentation at a local high school. The teacher had asked me to talk to her food systems class about being an organic farmer. After I finished my talk the teacher turned to her class. *So,* she asked, *how many of you think you might consider a career in agriculture after high school?*

Not a single student raised a hand.

The teacher surveyed the air above her students' heads for a few moments as if scanning the ocean for whales, as if any minute a hand might spring up. None did. Then she looked to me and offered a sympathetic half-smile, half-grimace, as if the tally had come in and I'd just lost an election.

> *"The large sums of capital that corporations can raise allow them to take advantage of economies of scale."*

Corporate Farming Is More Economically Efficient than Family Farming in Most Circumstances

Nathan Wittmaack

In the following viewpoint, Nathan Wittmaack provides an interesting history of farming and points out many of the problems with corporate farming, including the damage to rural culture, the concentration of power, and both humanitarian and environmental concerns. However, he concludes that limiting corporate farming is not the best way to address these issues. While economics of scale available to large farming operations are necessary, he does say that family farms can find opportunities in emerging markets for organic food. Wittmaack is the chief operating officer for an Iowa manufacturer of fertilizer blending and handling equipment.

"Should Corporate Farming Be Limited in United States?: An Economic Perspective," by Nathan Wittmaack. Reprinted by permission.

As you read, consider the following questions:

1. Wittmaack lists several disadvantages to corporate farming. Why does this not change his conclusion?
2. Beyond economies of scale, what other economic advantages does Wittmaack say corporate farms have?
3. In what circumstances does Wittmaack say family farms might be economically successful?

ABSTRACT

Farming in the United States has changed drastically over the last century. Technology has improved farmers' ability to produce. Economies of scale available from new technology have led to restructuring in the agricultural industry. Fewer and larger farms are now the norm. As technology improved, corporations began to increase activity in agricultural sectors. Sectors such as livestock are more susceptible to corporate farming. Many Americans are opposed to corporate farming because of the perceived negative effects on rural America. Limiting corporate farming, though, is not a good way to protect rural America. Corporate farming leads to a more efficient industry and more social benefits. This paper identifies the alleged negative effects of corporate farming, why it is occurring, and why it should not be opposed.

I. Introduction

In 1920 there were approximately 6.5 million farms in the United States. 30.1 percent of the population lived on farms. In 1992 those numbers were down to 2 million farms and less than 2 percent of the population living on farms [Allen and Lueck, 1998, 344].

The farming industry of today bears little resemblance to that of yesterday. Corporate farming has challenged the age-old structure of farming. Proponents of corporate farming say that it is more efficient than family farming and leads to more affordable food supplies. Opponents say the difference in efficiency does not justify the damage done to the rural way of life. Should agricultural states oppose corporate farming? Using economic theory, reasoning, and research, the paper concludes that corporate farming is economically more efficient than family farming in some circumstances. The assumption that corporate farming is a significant factor in the decrease of family farms is challenged as well.

II. Background

Since the Industrial Revolution, corporations have proven to be the most advantageous form of the industrial firm. The large sums of capital that corporations can raise allow them to take advantage of economies of scale. Corporations also enjoy limited liability. Henry Ford perfected a key ingredient to industrial efficiency. The assembly line made it easier to realize economies of scale. Economies of scale are the decreased costs per additional unit of input due to synergies in production. As production volume increases, the initial cost can be divided among more units of output. The assembly line is based on gains from specialization. As industry became more mechanized, it required fewer people to produce the same amount. It was, and still is, rare for an individual to own the resources required to capture substantial economies of scale. The corporate form of ownership is most able to capture economies of scale from industrialization.

Historically, agriculture has retained the "family firm" structure to a greater degree than other industries. Allen and Lueck suggest that this is largely due to the seasonality and randomness of nature and "the interplay of these qualities generates moral hazard, limits the gains from specialization, and causes timing problems between stages of production [1998, 343]." Agricultural sub-sectors experience different specialization and timing problems. For example, soybean farming must be done in a strict order and time frame that corresponds to natural seasons. Hog farming, though, takes place almost entirely indoors and is not as affected by natural cycles or variables. Government subsidies have allowed some types of family farmers to remain in the industry.

Corporate influence in farming has grown over the past 30 years. Not surprisingly, it has grown the most in sectors not as affected by natural cycles. The number of family farms in grain crop production has dropped over this period. The drop in family farms has not been due to corporate farming so much as the increasing size of the family farm. Many rural citizens blame the decrease in family farms on the increase in corporate farms. There are many arguments that have been made against corporate farming; they are discussed in section III. Opponents of corporate farming have responded by calling for legislation to prevent it.

Several Midwestern states have taken legislative steps to slow the spread of corporate farming. The first significant step in anti-corporate legislation occurred in the mid-1970s. In 1974, South Dakota enacted the Family Farm Act [Pietila, 2001, 153]. Iowa followed suit in 1975 with Iowa Code Chapter 9H.2 that prevents meatpackers from raising livestock [Vogel, 2004, 201]. Since that time, there have been various attempts by Midwestern states to legislate against corporate farming. The main thrust of the legislation has been to make it illegal for corporations to own multiple stages of production. The constitutionality of some of this legislation has been called into question recently. The 8th circuit United States District Court of Appeals recently repealed certain family farming acts in South Dakota [McDonough, 2003, 18]. Iowa's protectionist law was struck down as well by the United States District Court in the Southern District of Iowa [Vogel, 2004, 200]. These rulings were made on the basis of the dormant Commerce Clause found in Article One Section 8 of the U.S. Constitution. The dormant Commerce Clause limits the power of states to discriminate against out of state economic interests [Vogel, 2004, 209].

III. Arguments Against Corporate Farming

There are several hypothetical negative effects of corporate farming. There are many fewer family farms now than seventy years ago. Rural Americans, and others, are concerned that the decreasing number of family farms is harming the rural economy. Many rural Americans worry that corporate farming erodes their economy and their culture. Some people believe that vertical integration in food markets leads to a dangerous concentration of power over our food stock [Lyson and Welsh, 2005, 1489]. Remaining family farmers worry about access to markets. Others believe the savings of economies of scale in certain agricultural markets are not benefiting the consumer. Finally, some fear that corporate farming poses an unnecessary threat to the environment.

A. DECREASE IN NUMBER OF FAMILY FARMS

As explained in section II, the number of family farms and the population living on farms has declined drastically over the last 80 years. In 1933 there were approximately 6.5 million farms in the U.S.; in 2000 there were approximately 2 million [Tweeten, 2002, 1]. Opponents of corporate farming claim that the commercial corporate farming approach is a cause of the decline in family farms. Residents see corporate farming interests expand and believe it is driving out family farmers.

B. RURAL ECONOMY FEARS

The fear of a declining rural economy due to corporate farming is related to the decrease in the number of family farms. A study performed by Lyson and Welsh revealed rural economic problems associated with corporate farming. In the research, Lyson and Welsh conclude that corporate farming is associated with higher rates of unemployment and poverty [2005, 1487-1488].

As corporate farms continue to get larger, they will secure their inputs from centralized and standardized distributors [Lyson and Welsh, 2005, 1480]. Historically, the family farm did its agricultural business locally. This trade supported a huge number of agricultural businesses in rural communities. These businesses include grain elevators, community banks, farm supply stores, implement dealerships, seed dealers, and so on. Corporate farms do not rely on local resources like these; they secure their inputs and working capital from centrally located, large suppliers. If a corporate farm has fifty percent of the business in a rural area, the agriculture-related industry in that area has half as much business to support.

C. RURAL CULTURE FEARS

If the rural economy begins to collapse, it would have substantial impact on the culture in rural America. Small towns dominate the countryside of rural America, and many farmsteads dot the expanse between towns (though many fewer than 70 years ago). Small towns in rural America exist to support the agriculture that takes place around them. Nearly everything in a small town revolves around agriculture, even if it seems unrelated. These communities are a very distinct part of America's culture. Time seems to have moved much slower in small town rural America. Here, values of honesty, perseverance, hard work, dedication, and Godliness are embraced as the ideal. Morning coffee is a ritual, as is Sunday morning church. This subculture of America is very unique, but some believe that it will be lost if corporate farming is able to progress unchecked.

D. CONCENTRATION OF POWER

When one organization, or small group of organizations, amasses increasingly larger proportions of a scarce resource, its control over the market for that resource becomes much more substantial. For example, there are only 47 Tucker cars currently in existence ["Tucker History," 3]. If each of the Tuckers were in different individual's possessions, any one of them would sell for market value, and no individual owner would be able to influence the market price. If someone owned 45 of the existing 47 Tuckers, he would be able to control the market for Tucker cars. They could demand a premium because of the power they have in the market for Tuckers. This is the very concept that farm families are worried about. In the swine industry, the largest four companies control 60 percent of the market. 80 percent of the beef industry is controlled by the biggest four [McDonough, 2003, 18]. Vogel maintains that there is an alarmingly large discrepancy in power between meatpackers and independent producers. As this disparity in power grows, and the meatpackers continue to integrate with suppliers and buyers, the efficiency that they gain is unlikely to be passed on to consumers [2004, 207].

E. ACCESS TO MARKETS

The United States Supreme Court has said that the framers of the Constitution believed that every farmer should have access to every market in the country [Vogel, 2004, 200]. Corporate farms command a lot of market power. If a large corporate farm is integrated with a packer, all of the product will be channeled through that packer. The packer may not even accept product from farms that are not owned by or contracted with the corporation. In the past, a farmer was free to sell to the packer of his choice. The packer's ability to control its inputs by coordinating with its controlled farms eliminates its need to purchase that input from non-contract farmers.

The existence of the corporate meatpacker may put other area packers at risk. Corporation owned farms may have taken the place of family farms that previously split sales between more than one meatpacker. If the corporate farms all send their output to the corporate packer, it may put other packers out of business. Sales from farms that formerly had been divided would now all go to the corporate meatpacker. If these non-integrated packers cannot stay in business, it further decreases family farmer's access to markets.

F. ENVIRONMENTAL CONCERNS

The main environmental concerns about corporate farming come from large confinement operations. Brehm says that these operations are serious environmental threats to both water and air quality [2005, 811]. The shift from traditional livestock operations to large confinement operations is a result of the vertical integration of the livestock production system. As packers began contracting farmers to deliver set numbers of livestock in set time frames, banks began to loan against the contracts. Farmers then had access to enough capital to construct large, confinement operations [Brehm, 2005, 798].

The waste produced by large numbers of confined animals is the chief environmental concern. Applying the manure to farmland as fertilizer creates the possibility of runoff into neighboring water sources. Corporate farms often build lagoons, or large storage bunkers for waste. Lagoons present the problems of seepage and overflow [Brehm, 2005, 812]. Due to the sheer volume of waste, an inherent environmental danger exists. A water supply tainted by waste is undrinkable. Rivers, streams, ponds, and lakes contaminated with manure will not support the wildlife naturally found in them. Also, bacteria from the waste can make water unfit to swim in, reducing economic benefits associated with recreation.

Air pollution is another problem. Odors are created by livestock operations. The odor alone is enough to cause neighbors of a proposed confinement operation to protest. There is evidence that confinement operations pollute the air with harmful chemicals. Ammonia and hydrogen sulfide are present along with "volatile organic compounds" [Brehm 2005, 812].

G. HUMANITARIAN CONCERNS

Corporate farming depends on confinement-style operations. Humanitarian and moral questions are important issues to consider. In confinement style corporate farming operations, animals are allowed very little space to move. The animals do not live a natural life. It is not uncommon for animals to be physically harmed if they are weaker than the rest. Animal abuse happens as well. Often the farm managers do not care about any individual animal.

IV. A Discussion of Technological Change

Technological change has occurred rapidly over the last several decades. Improved technology has made it feasible for corporations to enter the farming industry. Many of the concerns about corporate farming are actually frustration about the double-edged sword of technological change. As technology has improved since the early 1900's, it has enabled farmers of all kinds to be more efficient. Tractors have replaced horses and oxen as means of production.

New alloys have led to larger and stronger equipment. Better technology means that farmers can extract more output from the same amount of input. The problem is that more efficiency means more output; more output means less revenue per unit of output due to the simple rules of supply and demand. In order to make up for the decrease in revenue per unit of output, costs of production must fall. The best way to make cost per unit of output to fall is to capture economies of scale (i.e. get bigger). A "vicious cycle" problem is apparent in this scenario with pressure to expand and produce more. In some agricultural sectors, corporations are most fit to handle this market.

A way to produce more is to buy more land, or find a way to jam all sorts of livestock into a small space. Technology has been the driver behind the failure of countless farms in the United States. Technology allows fewer people to farm more acres or livestock. Opponents of corporate farming who argue that it reduces the number of farms are trying to pin the tail on the wrong donkey. The very phenomenon (better technology) that has revolutionized farming for some has been the downfall of many others.

V. The Reach of Corporate Farming

The question arises, "is corporate farming a threat to every type of farmer?" After all, agriculture is a very broad concept in that it refers to all of the plant and livestock operations in the United States. Is corporate farming an issue in all types of farm operations? The short answer is, no. Virtually all of the research on corporate farming has been conducted on the livestock sector. Opponents of corporate farming tend not to make this distinction. Opposition to corporate farming is made on a broad, sweeping basis. Opponents would have you believe that corporate farms are prevalent in all types of farm business. In reality, corporate farming has affected grain crop farmers much less than livestock farmers. In 1992, only 1.3 percent of farm acreage was owned by corporate entities [Allen and Lueck, 1998, 343]. Acreage is a good measure of the presence of corporate farms in grain crop production. Raising livestock is no longer necessarily a land intensive practice, so its portion of the 1.3 percent of acreage is trivial.

Section IV discussed technology and how it has affected farming practices. It is technology that has changed the grain crop farm industry so much. Even if corporate farming were not an issue, farmers would continually be buying more land, squeezing other farmers out of the industry. It is much easier for grain crop farmers to put a face on the "enemy" by declaring that corporate farming is the culprit rather than the evolution of technology.

There are reasons why corporate farming has not embraced grain farming to this point. Some industries have attributes that lend themselves to a factory-style production process. Due to the advances in technology, there is little doubt that economies of scale exist in agriculture, no matter what sub-sector (livestock, grain, etc.). Economies of scale must exist for corporate farming to make sense.

Beyond economies of scale, gains from specialization are important in determining whether an industry can move to a factory-style corporate approach. It would be inefficient for farmers to divide up all of the jobs of grain production and each focus on one. The tasks in grain farming "...tend to be short, infrequent, and require few distinct tasks, thus limiting the benefits of specialization [Allen and Lueck, 1998, 344]." Grain crop farming is a repetitive process, but does not require a different skill set for each job.

Another factor that has delayed the onset of corporate farming is the uncertainty that exists within nature. Nature makes the move to factory-style corporate grain crop farms less likely in two ways. First, random shocks to output create a risk in farming. Drought, hail, and infestation are all possibilities. Individual farmers can insure their crops against seasonal disasters and seasonal shocks. Family farmers are compensated monetarily for their crop damage. Also, if the cause of the shock is widespread, the total supply of grain would be low, which would mean that the price would be relatively high. In general, corporations are well equipped to handle risk. Corporations, though, face a different risk in grain crop production. The corporately owned grain farm is a vertically integrated part of a production process. An important part of a production process is having consistent and reliable input flows. The relative uncertainty of grain farming does not provide a reliable input flow.

Second, grain farming is characterized by natural seasons that require certain production stages to take place at certain times [Allen and Lueck, 1998, 346]. Because of these factors, output from farm operations is limited to the end of natural cycles and the output may differ in quality or quantity from what was expected. A consistent and reliable input flow cannot be achieved because of the seasonality of grain farming.

Allen and Lueck explain that the sectors of agriculture that have been targeted by corporate farming are not random. Grain operations are particularly susceptible to the problems that nature presents.

> The general trend has been to remove stock from an open environment and rear them in climate-controlled barns... [N]ew technologies—in disease control, handling, nutrition, and transportation—have reduced seasonality by increasing the number of cycles per year...and reducing the importance and variability of random shocks from nature... Compared to field crops, livestock production allows for greater reduction of natural forces because stocks are mobile during growing stages and can often be reared indoors [Allen and Lueck, 1998, 370].

The implications of Allen and Lueck's paper are important. Corporate farming will not affect agricultural sectors that are characterized by random shocks to output and strictly seasonal nearly as much as sectors that are not affected. According to Allen and Lueck, grain crop operations should not have to worry about the onset of corporate farming.

Livestock farming, according to Allen and Lueck, is ideal for factory-style corporate farming because of the ability of technology to reduce the variability of the forces of nature on livestock production [1998, 379]. The move to corporate livestock farms was predicted by sound economic modeling and theory. It would be helpful if discussions on corporate farming were clearer about what types of farming are affected. There is little evidence that corporate farming has a serious interest in grain crop farming in the United States.

VI. Reasons for Corporate Farming

As explained in section IV, when an industry can be made more efficient from specialization and economies of scale, factory-style corporate industry will take hold. Livestock farmers have been able to all but eliminate the role that nature plays in production. Increases in technology and process innovation have allowed livestock farmers to extract a reliable and steady flow of output. It makes sense that livestock farming is an investment opportunity for corporations.

Open markets allocate resources most efficiently. The movement towards corporate farming in livestock production has happened because of market forces. Corporations can secure their inputs (the livestock) through high volume and highly reliable contracts. The corporation can then produce a consistent amount of output and can capitalize on economies of scale if they have a guaranteed flow of input. Factory-style corporate structured farms can produce more output for less money. The market rewards efficiency. According to Persaud and Tweeten, the real price of beef and pork (CPI-adjusted) decreased from 1980 to 1995. The producer price index (PPI-adjusted) has fallen as well, but at a slower rate. These differences in rates mean that there is a smaller margin on each unit of output of meat [2002, 128]. Decreased margins clearly show that the efficiency gains from corporate factory-style production are being passed on to consumers. The ability of corporate ownership to take advantage of economies of scale makes it the best choice for livestock production.

When an industry gravitates towards fewer but larger firms there is a tradeoff. That tradeoff is between the effects of market power and economies of scale. If the gains from economies of scale are greater than the loss to market power, the shift in the industry is beneficial [Persaud and Tweeten, 2002, 127]. In the above paragraph, it was noted that margins in the livestock industry have decreased. In the same time period that margins decreased (1980-1995), corporate farming really began to take hold. If fears about the market power of corporate farms distorting markets are legitimate, margins would not have declined. One reason corporate farms are integrating throughout the production process is to take advantage of task specialization. In order for a corporate farm to operate well, it must "...have farm products at the right time, place, quantity, quality, and price to process and meet consumers' demand [Persaud and Tweeten, 2002, 140-141]." These reforms in the livestock industry are in response to changes in technology that allow for efficiently coordinating the entire production process.

Scale economies that can be realized through new technology are a threat to the family farm structure that has dominated agriculture for so long. More animals can be farmed with less labor and more capital. In some situations (such as livestock, where nature can be mitigated) corporate farming has been the best choice. The scale economies and efficiency gains have led to large increases in national income that have benefited farmers in the long run [Persaud and Tweeten, 2002, 141]. Corporations have an advantage when securing markets and marketing products. This advantage in marketing not only increased demand nationally, but can increase global demand. Corporations are better suited to the challenges of a global economy. Traditional agriculture would have a much more difficult time capitalizing on the global economy.

VII. Discussion on Government

Any discussion on the agriculture industry must address the government's presence. The government has subsidized farm income and commodity prices for decades. Between 1950 and 2000, $451 billion was spent on farm subsidies [Tweeten, 2002, 1]. The government subsidies are meant to protect farmers from a market that was not believed to work. Natural production shocks, overproduction and high land prices are all problems that farmers have to deal with. The government tries to reduce the affects of these problems by subsidizing income, controlling supply, and offering relief.

The United States government has played a role in allowing the family farm to remain to this point. As information is more readily available, and as farms become larger, it is becoming clear that allowing the market work and ceasing subsidies is the best way to go [Tweeten, 2002, 1]. Whether or not to subsidize farms is not at issue. Contrary to common belief, subsidies tend to be awarded to very large farms. As a result, government subsidies are sometimes referred to as "corporate welfare." The largest grain farming operations receive the largest subsidies.

Perhaps the presence of government programs is one reason why there is a corporate presence (albeit limited) in grain farming. Government farm subsidy is a complex topic that deserves its own research. Subsidies' effect on the presence of corporate farming is very difficult to quantify. I can not offer a hypothesis on the direct effect of subsidies on the corporate farming trend. Its affect on livestock operations, the main bastion of corporate farming, is clearly limited.

VIII. Discussion on Negative Externalities

Negative externalities are costs of production that are not reflected in the price. Negative externalities result in overproduction of a product because not all of the costs are paid by the producer. The result is that others have to bear the cost of the externalities. Some concerns about corporate farming are based on fears of negative externalities. The efficient amount of corporate farming must have negative externalities internalized by the farms [Tweeten, 1997, 4]. What are the negative externalities associated with corporate farming?

Section III discussed arguments against corporate farming. Some of these arguments have been addressed in the preceding sections. The decrease in the number of farms can be accounted for almost entirely by the advances of technology in agriculture. Corporate farming has little to do with this problem, and has merely capitalized on the trend to move to a more efficient process with fewer farms.

Section V addressed the complaint that corporate farming puts too much power in the hands of too few. While more power does rest with vertically integrated corporate farming operations, there is not yet evidence that it has resulted in abuse of the power.

The most important negative externalities in corporate farming are its affects on rural economies and culture, as well as environmental and humanitarian concerns. As discussed in section III, as corporate entities take over farming and integrate stages of production, they will tend to acquire inputs from centralized locations that are not necessarily in close proximity to the farm operation itself. For example, a large corporate farm may do all of its borrowing at a large commercial bank rather than from the local loan officer. The corporate farm will also purchase all of its farming supplies from venders (possibly) not associated with the local economy. If a corporate farming operation takes the place of what was once several family farming operations, the businesses that rely on farmers to support them would not be able to keep their doors open. The rural economy is primarily based on the existence of small farming towns and the agribusiness that happens within those towns.

It is not surprising that agriculture-based small towns in the Midwest have seen a large drop in population. The population decline is partially due to the existence of corporate farms procuring operating resources from large markets that are unrelated to the local rural economy. As the rural economy goes, so does the rural culture. Small agricultural towns are the hub of rural culture in the United States. If the towns suffer, so will the rural culture.

It is important to note that it is extremely unclear as to what extent corporate farming has contributed to the decline of the rural economy and culture. This paper has identified technology as the primary force in agricultural changes. Because technological change can have the same effect on communities and culture as corporate farming, it is difficult to assign any concrete portion solely to corporate farming.

Environmental concerns are valid in corporate farming. Air and water pollution are big hurdles for large scale corporate farming operations. But, the same problems are present whether the operating structure is corporate or not. The shear numbers of animals housed in a relatively small area cause the problem. Nearly the same argument can be made for the humanitarian problem. Once again, it is difficult to put a price on the effect of the environmental negative externality.

Opinions exist on both sides of the environmental question. Some maintain that if corporations had to account for their negative environmental externalities, then corporate-style production would not be the most efficient way of farming [Brehm, 2005, 799]. Others believe that corporate structure in farming would be the most efficient even if they did internalize all external costs. There are also ways to reduce the amount of negative externalities. Locating in remote areas where rural economies do not already exist would reduce the affects on established rural economies, and negate the problem of air pollution [Tweeten, 1997, 4]. Humanitarian issues are even more difficult to discuss, but would do little to affect the market choice of corporate farming.

IX. Conclusions

This paper has discussed the changing landscape of agriculture. Corporate farming is becoming more prevalent; some are very concerned by the effects of this shift. Most of the perceived negative effects of corporate farming in the United States can actually be attributed to technological change. The technological change has given corporations the ability to expand into agriculture, especially livestock, and produce more efficiently. Natural shocks and cycles can be negated by technology. Vertical integration by corporations is the best and most efficient way to capture the economies of scale and gains from specialization available.

Rural communities are dying; there is little argument about that. The number of farms and the corresponding population has decreased drastically over the last 70 years. Can corporate farming damage the rural culture even more? Because of the nature of grain farming, there is little chance that corporations will embrace grain production like they have livestock. Nature maintains a huge role in grain production. Unless technology makes it possible for producers to standardize grain output like it has livestock output, there will likely be little interest in corporate grain farming.

Negative externalities are important to consider, and more research should be done to develop a model that internalized all of the costs of corporate farming. It will be difficult to separate the negative externalities attributed to the existence of corporate farms with those associated with technological progress. If the gains from corporate farming outweigh its externalities, as it appears that they do, it should continue to exist.

If it is determined that limiting corporate farming is a good method to use in preserving the rural American culture, and society values that more than more efficient production, corporate farming should be limited by states. But even though society may value rural American culture over lower prices, limiting corporate-style farming is probably not the way to protect it. Instead, technology would have to be intentionally limited, and probably reduced. It appears that the American rural culture is in decline, and limiting corporate farming will probably not stop it. Agricultural states should not oppose corporate farming, unless new research discovers the negative externalities of corporate farming (and not technological change) outweigh the benefits they produce.

Hope exists for rural culture in the United States. Family farms have the opportunity to seek out niche markets that may bring premium prices. Premium prices may offset their forgone benefit of being larger and more efficient (capturing economies of scale). Organic markets are one possibility. Demand exists for organic foods; small family farmers may find that they are best equipped to capture the market. The technology that makes farms more efficient is often from genetic alteration and is heavily reliant on chemicals. Capturing economies of scale is more difficult without the use of these technologies, and may leave the door open for small farmers.

References

Allen, Douglas W., and Lueck, Dean (1998), "The Nature of the Farm," *Journal of Law and Economics*, 41, n2: 343-386.

Brehm, Susan M. (2005), "From Red Barn to Facility: Changing Environmental Liability to Fit Changing Structure of Livestock Production," *California Law Review*, 93:797-846.

Lyson, Thomas A., and Welsh, Rick (2005), "Agricultural industrialization, anticorporate farming laws, and rural community welfare," *Environment and Planning A*, 37: 1479-1491.

McDonough, Molly (2003), "Down on the Farm," *ABA Journal*, 89: 18-20.

Persaund, Suresh, and Tweeten, Luther (2002), "Impact of Agribusiness Market Power on Farmers" in Tweeten, Luther and Thompson, Stanley R., *Agricultural Policy for the 21st Century*. Ames, IA: Iowa State Press.

Pietila, John C. (2001), ""[W]e're Doing This to Ourselves": South Dakota's Anticorporate Farming Amendment," *Journal of Corporation Law*, 27, 1: 149-172.

Tucker History, *The Tucker Automobile Club of America*, http://www.tuckerclub.org/html/history.php.

Tweeten, Luther (1997), "Agricultural Industrialization, For Better or Worse?" *Ohio State University*, http://www-agecon.ag.ohio- state.edu/programs/Anderson/papers_old/Agricultural%20Industrialization— For%20Better%20or%20Worse.pdf.

Tweeten, Luther (2002), "Farm Commodity Programs: Essential Safety Net or Corporate Welfare?" in Tweeten, Luther and Thompson, Stanley R., *Agricultural Policy for the 21st Century*. Ames, IA: Iowa State Press.

Vogel, Jennifer M. (2004), "Iowa Code Chapter 9H.2: The State of Iowa's Battle Against Corporate Farming," *Journal of Corporation Law,* 30, 1: 199-218.

Periodical and Internet Sources Bibliography

The following articles have been selected to supplement the diverse views presented in this chapter.

Olga Bonfiglio, "The Economics of Organic Farming," CommonDreams.org, May 9, 2010.

Karen J. Coates, "The Global Land Grab: Big Countries Are Buying Up Poor Countries," *Slate*, April 25, 2014. http://www.slate.com /articles/health_and_science/feed_the_world/2014/04/land_ grab_in_the_developing_world_big_agriculture_will_make_ more_people.html.

Economist, "Against the Grain: The Fad for the Andean Staple Has Not Hurt the Poor—Yet," May 21, 2016. http://www.economist .com/news/finance-and-economics/21699087-fad-andean-staple -has-not-hurt-pooryet-against-grain?zid=293&ah=e50f636873b4 2369614615ba3c16df4a.

Chris Hunt, "How to Slap Big Ag Apologists in the Face with Economic Truth," Gracelinks.org, June 23, 2012. http://gracelinks .org/blog/1067/how-to-slap-big-ag-apologists-in-the-face-with -economic-tru.

Betsy Isaacson, "To Feed Humankind, We Need the Farms of the Future Today," *Newsweek*, October 22, 2015. http://www .newsweek.com/2015/10/30/feed-humankind-we-need-farms -future-today-385933.html.

Gracy Olmstead, "Down on the Farm: Small Farmers Face Regulatory Burdens, Negative Sterotypes, and Children Fleeing the Family Business," *National Review*, August 15, 2016. http://www .nationalreview.com/article/438983/small-farms-big-business -family-farms-struggle-against-industrial-agriculture.

Tom Philpott, "Robots Are Growing Tons of Our Food. Here's the Creepy Part (It's Not What You Think)," Mother Jones, September/October 2016.

Matthew Prescott, "Your Pig Almost Certainly Came from a Factory Farm, No Matter What Anyone Tells You," *Washington Post*, July 15, 2014. https://www.washingtonpost.com/posteverything /wp/2014/07/15/your-pig-almost-certainly-came-from

-a-factory-farm-no-matter-what-anyone-tells-you/?utm_
term=.336b279a4e47.

Vincent H. Smith and Robert Goodman, "Should Washington End
Agricultural Subsidies?" *Wall Street Journal*, July 12, 2015. http://
www.wsj.com/articles/should-washington-end-agriculture
-subsidies-1436757020.

Tom Szaky, "The Economics of Organic," *Huffington Post*, July 14,
2016. http://www.huffingtonpost.com/tom-szaky/the-economics
-of-organic_b_10971738.html.

OPPOSING
VIEWPOINTS®
SERIES

CHAPTER 4

Is Corporate Farming Morally Justifiable?

Chapter Preface

Throughout this book, you've read arguments about the environmental and economic sustainability of corporate farming, and whether or not large-scale, corporate, industrial farming is necessary to feed the world's rapidly increasing population. For the most part, these have been practical arguments: monocultures and pesticides do long-term damage to the environment; high-tech farming techniques are both safe and necessary; large-scale farming is a looming economic disaster; small-scale farming is not economically feasible.

But embedded in these practical arguments is a rather more difficult question: Is corporate, industrial farming morally justifiable? If the methods and practices of this type of farming do in fact harm the environment and potentially damage the health of people who harvest the crops and eat the food grown in this way, then does that mean that the practice is immoral? Many of the voices we have heard so far in this book would likely say that it is. Of course many believe that even if large-scale farming is as harmful as its critics claim (a view that is, as we have seen, disputed by many), the benefits—providing cheap food for billions of people who might otherwise starve—outweigh the damage, perhaps even turning an immoral act into a moral necessity. Others believe that that premise is itself false: corporate farming isn't actually feeding the world and contributes to inequalities in wealth and resources that lead to poverty and therefore hunger.

Those who defend the morality of corporate farming often focus on what is one of the more contentious aspects of modern agriculture: genetically modified crops. Not only do supporters claim that GMO crops are safe to both human and environmental health, they point out that the judicious use of bio-technology in farming can reduce other harms, for example by reducing the need for pesticides and providing nutrient-enhanced staple grains to malnourished populations.

In this final chapter, we shall see several viewpoints that address, either directly or more subtly, the question of how morally justifiable is corporate, industrial farming. One article focuses entirely on the legality of the claims, while others parse the science and the public's understanding of it. One addresses animal cruelty, while others question the honesty of industry-supported researchers. But running underneath and throughout all these viewpoints is the question of whether it is better to run some risks to ensure that nine billion people have enough food to eat, or run some risks to ensure that those nine billion people are fed safely.

| "*The NR and the National Academy of Science take millions of dollars in funding from corporations like Monsanto, DuPont, and Dow Chemical.*"

Those Who Say GMOs Are Safe to Eat Are Not Objective

Nadia Prupis

In the following viewpoint, Nadia Prupis argues that we must consider the motives of research organizations before accepting their recommendations. In chapter two we saw that many scientists have determined that genetically modified organisms are safe for the environment (and human health as well). In that article, the author reported that scientists had posted their findings online and were asking the public to take a look and make their own judgments. Here we have a viewpoint saying that the scientists who claim that GMOs are safe to eat receive money from the industry that produces and markets GMOs, potentially influencing their evaluation of the data. Prupis is a staff writer for Common Dreams, a progressive news outlet.

"GMOs Safe to Eat, Says Research Group That Takes Millions From Monsanto," by Nadia Prupis, Common Dreams, May 18, 2016. http://www.commondreams.org/news/2016/05/18/gmos-safe-eat-says-research-group-takes-millions-monsanto. Licensed under CC BY-SA 3.0.

As you read, consider the following questions:

1. How might knowing that the scientists who did the studies were potentially biased influence your own evaluation of the evidence?

2. What is the conflict of interest Prupis describes, and why might that influence the content of the report?

3. What is one suggestion in this article for reducing the conflict of interest?

P ublic skepticism is growing over a new report that claims genetically modified (GE or GMO) foods are safe for consumption, particularly as information emerges that the organization that produced the report has ties to the biotechnology industry.

Genetically Engineered Crops: Experiences and Prospects, released Tuesday by the federally-supported National Academies of Sciences, Engineering, and Medicine, states not only that GMO crops are safe to eat, but that they have no adverse environmental impacts and have cut down on pesticide use. Its publication comes as U.S. Congress—which founded the institution—considers making GMO labeling mandatory on consumer products.

"There clearly are strong non-safety arguments and considerable public support for mandatory labeling of products containing GE material. The committee does not believe that mandatory labeling of foods with GE content is justified to protect public health," the report states.

However, one day before publication, the environmental advocacy group Food & Water Watch (FWW) reported in an issue brief that the National Research Council (NRC)—the National Academy of Sciences' research arm—has deep ties to the biotech and agricultural industries, which FWW says have "created conflicts of interests at every level of the organization."

The NRC and the National Academy of Science take millions of dollars in funding from corporations like Monsanto, DuPont, and Dow Chemical, FWW reported in its issue brief, *Under the Influence: The National Research Council and GMOs* .

Representatives from those companies—along with Cargill, General Mills, and Nestlé Purina, among other GMO-friendly businesses—also sit on the NRC's board that oversees GMO projects. NRC has not publicly disclosed those ties, FWW said. In fact, more than half of the invited authors of the new report have ties to the industry.

According to the issue brief, not only does the NRC have a history of bias toward the industry, it has also worked to silence critics of GMOs and of the companies that sit on its board.

"While companies like Monsanto and its academic partners are heavily involved in the NRC's work on GMOs, critics have long been marginalized," said Wenonah Hauter, FWW executive director. "Many groups have called on the NRC many times to reduce industry influence, noting how conflicts of interest clearly diminish its independence and scientific integrity."

The issue brief states:

> Weak, watered-down or biased findings from the NRC have a very real impact on our food system. Policy makers develop "science-based" rules and regulations on GMOs based on what the science says—especially what the NRC says, because it is part of the National Academy of Sciences, chartered by Congress to provide scientific advice to the federal government.
>
> And this is where science can become politicized. Companies like Monsanto need favorable science and academic allies to push their controversial products through regulatory approval and on to American farms. Corporate agribusinesses pour millions of dollars into our public universities, play a heavy hand in peer-reviewed scientific journals and seek to influence prestigious scientific bodies like the National Research Council.

Despite these criticisms, the NRC has continued to cover up its connections to agribusiness and the true influence the industry wields over its research.

"Under the Federal Advisory Committee Act, the NRC is required to form balanced committees of scientists to carry out its research—and to disclose any conflicts of interest," Hauter continued. "Yet the NRC failed to disclose even the conflicts of the members of this deeply unbalanced committee."

In its issue brief, FWW called for specific changes to combat industry influence:

- Congress should expand and enforce the Federal Advisory Committee Act to ensure that the scientific advice the NRC produces for the government is free of conflicts of interest and bias;
- Congress should immediately halt all taxpayer funding for agricultural projects at the NRC until meaningful conflicts-of-interest policies are enforced;
- The NRC should no longer engage funders, directors, authors or reviewers that have a financial interest in the outcome of any of the NRC's work; and
- The NRC should prohibit the citation of science funded or authored by industry, given the obvious potential for bias.

"Agribusiness companies like Monsanto have an outsized role at our public universities, at peer-reviewed journals, and the NRC," Hauter concluded. "We won't have good public policy on new technologies like GMOs until these rampant conflicts of interest are exposed."

> *"None of these studies proves or even persuasively suggests that GMOs can be harmful to human health. The majority are either obviously flawed or are not scientific studies."*

Opposition to Genetically Engineered Foods Is Based on Bad Science and Dishonest Hype

Layla Katiraee

In the following viewpoint, Layla Katiraee directly addresses ten studies and the subsequent claims by anti-GMO groups about the health hazards of genetically engineered food. She looks at several of the studies cited and linked by anti-GMO articles on the web, and challenges the logic and/or the scientific methods of each of them. According to Katiraee, much of the opposition to genetically modified foods is based on at the very least sloppy and often deceptive material masquerading as legitimate scientific research. Katiraee is a molecular biologist and senior scientist with a biotechnology firm in California.

"10 Studies Proving GMOs Are Harmful? Not if Science Matters," by Layla Katiraee, The Genetic Literacy Project, November 13, 2015. Reprinted by permission.

As you read, consider the following questions:

1. Why is a "pay-for-play" journal?

2. How does the author say news media misreported the study on cancer cells and glyphosate?

3. What are peer-reviewed studies, and why are they so important?

Activists often cite the alleged potential health risks of genetically modified foods. One recent example of this—"10 Scientific Studies Proving GMOs Can Be Harmful To Human Health," posted on Collective-Evolution.com—outlines many familiar concerns and points in each case to "credible scientific studies that clearly demonstrate why GMOs should not be consumed."

Are these concerns credible? What do the studies cited actually claim?

1) Multiple Toxins From GMOs Detected In Maternal and Fetal Blood.

The blog post sites a 2010 study that alleges to show this danger. The authors identified the *Bt* protein Cry1Ab in maternal and fetal blood, a protein found in some GMOs, but also commonly used as a pesticide in organic farming. The paper is flawed. The researchers' measurements were based on an experiment/assay designed to detect *Bt*'s Cry1Ab in plants, not in humans. As this post in Biofortified.org explains, the pregnant women in the study would have had to eat several kilos of corn in order to get the Bt measurements that were detected in their blood.

Additionally, there's the "so what" factor. Humans lack the receptors for the protein, so it has no impact on us. Did you know that chocolate is toxic to dogs? Are you concerned that it might be toxic to you? Probably not (if you *are* concerned, then you've missed out on the greatest source of joy known to human taste buds…). Some chemical compounds behave differently among species, and both *Bt*'s Cry1Ab and chocolate are examples of this.

2) DNA From Genetically Modified Crops Can Be Transferred Into Humans Who Eat Them

That's not what the cited 2013 study concluded. The authors found that whole genes from our food can be detected in our plasma. That does not mean that they've integrated into our DNA; it means that they've been found floating in the space between cells. And that's any food, not just GMOs. DNA from GMOs behave no differently than DNA from organic or conventional foods.

If you aren't concerned about the DNA from blueberries "transferring" into you, then you should not be concerned about DNA from GMOs either. The paper's deepest flaw is that a negative control was not included in the sequencing experiments. Several recent papers have outlined the importance of including a negative control in experiments where there is very little DNA to account for possible contaminants from the environment and reagents.

3) New Study Links GMOs to Gluten Disorders That Affect 18 Million Americans

The article quotes from an alleged "study" by the Institute for Responsible Technology (IRT). But there is no study on the link of GMOs to gluten allergies. There's a link to a post on a webpage, but there isn't a peer-reviewed article. IRT is a one-man band run by activist Jeffrey Smith. It is an NGO that advocates for the elimination of GMOs from our food supply. It's not a university, college or research institution. It doesn't do studies.

I've written about gluten allergies and GMOs. The Celiac Disease foundation has spoken out against the IRT's report. GMO wheat has not been commercialized, so any association of gluten allergies with the consumption of GMO wheat is on its face absurd. As for charts that track an increase in GMO consumption in general and gluten allergies, it's a case of association with no causation (i.e. the incidence of gluten allergies has increased over the past decade and the amount of GMOs we eat has increased too. But, so have the number of plasma screens manufactured).

4) Study Links Genetically Modified Corn to Rat Tumors

This claim is the infamous Seralini paper, which was retracted, and recently republished, in a different journal without being peer reviewed. The paper identified tumors in rats that were fed GMOs and/or the herbicide glyphosate longterm. But the strain of rat used was predisposed to tumors. The paper did not perform statistical analyses and used too few rats, so it was not possible to determine if the tumors were due to the food, the chemical or to the fact that the strain of rats would get tumors regardless of what they were fed. Finally, the findings from Seralini's paper are contrary to other long-term feeding studies.

5) Glyphosate Induces Human Breast Cancer Cells Growth via Estrogen Receptors

This claim relates to glyphosate, an herbicide used in tandem with herbicide resistant genetically modified crops. The cited paper examines the impact of glyphosate on breast cancer cell growth. In approximately 80 percent of instances of breast cancer, the diseased cells are hormone sensitive, meaning they need estrogen in order to proliferate and spread. These researchers took two breast cancer cell lines: one was estrogen sensitive and one was not, and they examined the impact of increasing amounts of glyphosate on cell growth. They found that glyphosate has similar impact on breast cancer growth as estrogen, although the relationship was not as strong, and it did not have an impact on the proliferation of the non-hormone sensitive breast cancer cell line.

The paper had numerous technical problems, including the absence of data on controls, a potentially critical omission. Additionally, there actually seems to be a protective effect at higher concentrations of glyphosate: instead of reaching a saturation point where the addition of glyphosate no longer has an effect on cell growth, there is no significant difference in cellular growth between the cells that received the highest doses of glyphosate and the controls (which is why the data from the controls is an important factor).

This experiment was done with cells in a petri dish—what's called an *in vitro* tissue-culture experiment. Such research is of limited real-world value. The cells are often finicky and need plenty of TLC in order to grow well; different cell lines can also behave very differently. The authors of the paper note some of these issues, along with the fact that their data doesn't mesh with previous studies that have examined the impact of glyphosate on cellular proliferation (this previous paper suggests that glyphosate actually *protects* against cell proliferation *in vitro* in eight different cancer cell lines and that glyphosate might be developed into an anti-cancer drug!).

Monsanto wrote a response to the paper noting that many studies examined the potential carcinogenicity of glyphosate and none has found that the compound causes cancer. Some news reports misinterpreted the study, writing that researchers concluded that glyphosate causes cancer when that is *not* the researchers' findings: they *suggest* glyphosate *may* cause breast cancer to *proliferate*. Monsanto pointed out that even this finding is contrary to the body of evidence that exists on the topic. The authors admit to this fact and discuss the appropriate next steps to examine this issue in mice/rats models for breast cancer. I think that that's a great next step. I'd also look at a few more breast-cancer cell lines.

This is the most compelling research paper that I've read about that suggests a *potential* health risk surrounding glyphosate. But the study must be reproduced and its issues ironed out. However, as I mentioned, the paper isn't really about GMOs as a class: keep in mind that only a fraction of GMOs are glyphosate resistant (i.e. Round-up Ready crops) and the use of glyphosate is not limited to GMOs.

Additionally, the paper does several experiments with a compound in soybean whose impact on breast cancer cell growth

Factory Farming Can Kill People

According the Centers for Disease Control and Prevention, animal products are the primary source of saturated fat in the American diet. Saturated fat has been linked to heart disease and obesity. Studies have shown that the unnatural feeds used to promote growth in animals on factory farms increase the saturated fat content of meat.

... The six growth hormones commonly used by the U.S. dairy industry have been shown to significantly increase the risk of breast, prostate, and colon cancer in beef consumers. Producers are not required to list the use of hormones on product labels.

... [A]n estimated 70 percent of the antibiotics used in the U.S. are given to farm animals for non-therapeutic purposes. Using antibiotics in this way can lead to drug-resistant bacteria; as a result, certain bacterial infections have already become or are on their way to becoming untreatable in humans. Antibiotic resistant infections kill 90,000 Americans every year.

Poor sanitation and waste management on factory farms and the poor management of animal waste can lead to the contamination of the food supply by bacteria like E.coli and salmonella. ....

Some diseases, like H1N1 (Swine Flu) and Avian Flu, are communicable from animals to humans. These "zoonotic" diseases have the potential to become pandemics. Experts believe that the outbreak of H1N1 was likely caused by the overcrowding of pigs on factory farms and the storage of their waste in giant manure lagoons.

"Factory Farming and Human Health." Farmsanctuary.

is very similar to that of glyphosate's—meaning that there are "natural" compounds in our food that seem to have the same impact on breast-cancer proliferation that this paper's findings suggest for glyphosate. There does not seem to be a scientific consensus on the topic of soy intake in breast cancer patients, although several publications have examined this issue without finding a positive correlation.

6) Glyphosate Linked to Birth Defects

No peer reviewed, published scientific study makes such claims. The source of this health concern is a publication by Earth Open Source, an anti-GMO NGO [non-governmental organization] co-founded by an individual who also owns a GMO-testing and certification company, and whose business would clearly benefit through the promotion of anti-GMO sentiments.

7) Study Links Glyphosate to Autism, Parkinson's and Alzheimer's

The paper that led to this health claim does not constitute research. It's a hypothesis and no research was done to support the hypothesis. The paper was reviewed by science journalist Keith Kloor at Discover Magazine who aptly compared it to a Glenn Beck chalkboard drawing.

The claims were printed in a pay-for-play journal (also known as predatory journal), meaning that for a fee, one can get nearly anything published. There have been several exposés on pay-for-play journals, and many scientists believe that the phenomenon is eroding the quality of science.

8) Chronically Ill Humans Have Higher Glyphosate Levels Than Healthy Humans

This claim is based on a paper published in the Journal of Environmental and Analytical Toxicology, owned by the Omics publishing group—a notorious predatory publishing company.

The authors examined glyphosate levels in humans and different animals. There's no indication of what the animals were fed, how much, how they were kept or myriad other variables. Any of these could invalidate the study. The researchers do not say anything about the age, sex, weight, height, or genetic background of the humans, or how much they ate, if they washed their food, how long they had been eating organic/conventional diets and, most mind-blowing of all, there's absolutely no definition for what constitutes being "chronically ill." Any single issue that I've listed here would be considered a fatal flaw that would exclude the paper from publication in a more prestigious journal.

9) Studies Link GMO Animal Feed to Severe Stomach Inflammation and Enlarged Uteri in Pigs

In the study on which this claim is based, the researchers gave pigs GMO feed and non-GMO feed and identified the differences between the two groups. The paper has been thoroughly challenged by many journalists and scientists:

- Journalist Mark Lynas highlighted the degree to which the data is cherry-picked. The difference in "inflammation" between the GM-fed and non-GM-fed pigs is apparent only when you break down the degree of inflammation into subcategories, but there's no difference if you view it as a single category. Overall, there's a high rate of inflammation for both groups, which is not explained in the paper. At the same time, there are several parameters where GM-feed could be argued as having a protective effect (there are 50 percent fewer heart-abnormalities in pigs fed GM-grain), but this isn't discussed.
- As explained by geneticist Anastasia Bodnar, the authors do not analyze the compositional differences in the feed between the two groups. Previous studies have determined that the environment (i.e., water, soil, geography) of a crop has a greater impact on proteins and metabolites than whether or not the crop is a GMO. As such, the differences seen in the pigs may not be due pesticides or presence/absence of the transgenic protein; rather, they are most likely due to differences in composition of the feed.
- Geneticist Val Giddings notes that the animals had abnormally high rates of pneumonia, which points to the possibility that something wonky was going on.

In conclusion, even if the paper's findings are real, there's no knowing whether that's due to something associated with transgenes or not, because the researchers do not account for natural variation in the feed.

10) GMO risk assessment is based on very little scientific evidence in the sense that the testing methods recommended are not adequate to ensure safety.

Let's set aside the fact that this isn't a "Scientific Study Proving GMOs Can Be Harmful To Human Health," which is the claim set out in the title. There are three papers associated with this bullet point. The first one is a review and I agree with a few of the points it makes. It highlights the need for *standardized* tests and statistics in animal feeding studies for GMOs, and anyone who followed the Seralini debacle would probably agree. It summarizes papers that have performed feeding studies and their results. However, the review does not remove flawed papers from their overview and nor does it distinguish between feeding studies for GMO crops that have been commercialized vs. crops that have never been submitted for regulatory approval. The paper does not conclude, "GMO risk assessment is based on very little scientific evidence."

The second paper is also a review piece. The first author is affiliated with "Friends of the Earth," an anti-GMO NGO. It does not constitute novel research and has a clear editorial slant.

The third paper does not even qualify as a review. It's a commentary published in 2002 in Nature Biotechnology, which is a high caliber journal. It outlined possible unintended consequences that *could* happen with a GMO—none of which have ever been documented or identified since then, to the best of my knowledge.

In conclusion, despite the title of the article, none of these studies proves or even persuasively suggests that GMOs can be harmful to human health. The majority are either obviously flawed or are not scientific studies.

The current scientific consensus regarding GMOs remains unchanged: they are safe and do not pose a health risk to humans. However, a scientific consensus is subject to change if there is sufficient *reproducible* evidence that may impact it, but none of the studies reviewed here constitute such evidence.

> *"Agricultural markets are now
> bracing for an explosion of new
> plants designed using the precise
> gene-editing technology CRISPR,
> and regulators in both the United
> States and the European Union are
> struggling with how to assess their
> safety."*

Genetically Engineered Crops Are Safe to Eat

Kelly Servick

*In the following viewpoint, Kelly Servick maintains that GMOs
are safe. But unlike in previous viewpoints, this author addresses
their safety as food. Here, she outlines the latest appraisal of the
research attesting to the safety of genetically modified crops and also
discusses problems with the regulatory process, as determined by that
research. The criteria used to classify GMOs is lagging behind the
science, according to this report. Servick is a staff writer for* Science,
*a publication of the American Association for the Advancement
of Science.*

"Once Again, U.S. Expert Panel Says Genetically Engineered Crops Are Safe to Eat," by
Kelly Servick, American Association for the Advancement of Science -AAAS, May 17,
2016. Reprinted by permission.

As you read, consider the following questions:

1. How, accordion to this article, do experts suggest that farmers manage the risk of pests evolving resistance to crops engineered to have their own pesticides?

2. How has new technology changed the definitions of genetically modified organisms and complicated the regulatory process?

3. What are the National Academies doing to help prevent this problem of occurring in the future?

Almost 2 years ago, a group of 20 scientists began hashing out a consensus on the risks and benefits of genetically engineered (GE) crops. Since the launch of their study, sponsored by the National Academies of Science, Engineering, and Medicine, the public debate around the safety of genetically modified organisms (GMOs) and whether to label them has continued to rage. But behind the scenes, some things have changed. Agricultural markets are now bracing for an explosion of new plants designed using the precise gene-editing technology CRISPR, and regulators in both the United States and the European Union are struggling with how to assess their safety.

The panel's report, released today, is a hefty literature review that tackles mainstay questions in the well-worn GMO debate. Are these plants safe to eat? How do they affect the environment? Do they drive herbicide-resistance in weeds or pesticide-resistance in insects? But it also weighs in on a more immediate conundrum for federal agencies: what to do with gene-edited plants that won't always fit the technical definition of a regulated GE crop.

The authors picked through hundreds of research papers to make generalizations about GE varieties already in commercial production: There is "reasonable evidence that animals were not harmed by eating food derived from GE crops," and epidemiological data shows no increase in cancer or any other health problems as a result of these crops entering into our food supply. Pest-resistant crops that poison insects thanks to a gene from the soil bacterium *Bacillus thuringiensis* (Bt) generally allow farmers to use less pesticide. Farmers can manage the risk of those pests evolving resistance by using crops with high enough levels of the toxin and planting non-Bt "refuges" nearby. Crops designed to be resistant to the herbicide glyphosate, meanwhile, can lead to heavy reliance on the chemical, and spawn resistant weeds that "present a major agronomic problem." The panel urges more research on strategies to delay weed resistance.

Few researchers will be surprised at those conclusions, says Todd Kuiken, who leads the Synthetic Biology Project at the Woodrow Wilson International Center for Scholars, a think tank in Washington, D.C., but public skepticism of GE crops runs deep. "Whether the academy kind of putting their seal of approval on that impacts the discussion, I don't know."

Regulatory muddle

The report saves the issue of regulation for its final chapter. Many countries—including the United States, whose framework for reviewing new biotechnology products was drafted in 1986—didn't envision modern technologies when they legally defined genetic engineering. The first generation of GE crops used a bacterium to ferry genes from one organism into another. But CRISPR can knockout or precisely edit DNA sequences without leaving behind any foreign DNA. In fact, the DNA of a gene-edited crop could end up looking nearly identical to that of a conventionally bred variety. Last month, the U.S. Department of Agriculture (USDA) deemed two CRISPR-edited crops, a mushroom that resists browning and a high-yield variety of waxy corn, to be exempt from its review process because neither contained genetic material from species considered to be "plant pests."

Critics of those decisions argue that small genetic changes can still have big effects on the characteristics of a plant, and that gene-edited crops have slipped through the cracks without proper safety testing. Others argue that the precision of CRISPR limits environmental and health risks by making fewer unintended tweaks to a plant's genome, and that subjecting them to a full regulatory review is needlessly costly and time consuming for their producers.

Last summer, the White House announced it would revamp the legal framework for evaluating biotechnology products across USDA, the Food and Drug Administration, and the Environmental Protection Agency (EPA). The European Commission, meanwhile, is also mulling whether plants without foreign DNA count as genetically modified.

Like several National Academies reviews before it, the new study condemned regulatory approaches that classify products based on the technology used to create them. "The National Academy has been saying since 1987 that it should be the product, not the process," says Fred Gould, an applied evolutionary biologist at North Carolina State University in Raleigh, and chair of the new report. "But the problem up until now is … how do you decide which products need more examination than others?"

There, the report makes a new suggestion: Regulators should ask for a full analysis of a plant's composition—using modern "-omics" tools such as genome sequencing and analysis of the proteins and small molecules in a sample—to determine when a full safety review is necessary. The authors propose that crops containing different genes, producing a different set of proteins, or carrying out different metabolic reactions than conventionally bred varieties should trigger regulatory review if those differences have potential health or environmental impacts. And if a trait is so new that there's no conventional counterpart to compare it to … just go ahead and regulate it, they conclude.

The approach is reasonable, Kuiken says, but it's not clear how to implement it. "How close does it have to be to the counterpart before you have to do a full review?"

Gould acknowledges that the report's recommendation is a tall order, but "if USDA and EPA don't use -omics techniques and they deregulate a crop, and then somebody in a research lab just takes a look at the transcriptome and finds a difference, you're in trouble." Deciding exactly which kinds of genetic or metabolic changes represent a risk will be left to regulatory agencies. "We just give principles," Gould adds. "We're not in the trenches with them."

If those entrenched regulators crave more guidance, they're in luck. The National Academies just launched yet another study, due out by the end of this year, to predict the next decade of biotechnology products and describe the scientific tools needed to regulate them.

> *"Rather than worrying about unsubstantiated risks from GMOs, Americans should worry about the real risks pesticides pose for people in the communities that feed the nation."*

Pesticides—not GMOs—Are Harming Farmworkers and Children in Rural Areas

Liza Gross

In the following viewpoint, Liza Gross agrees that GMOs have not been proven harmful to human health. She argues, however, that the real danger from corporate farming is pesticide use. All the attention given to GMO crops distracts public attention from the more serious danger in the food supply. Gross cites evidence from studies of mothers and children working in agricultural jobs or living near areas with high pesticide applications to support her claim that pesticide use interferes with the growth and development of children, resulting in many cases in lower IQs and delayed verbal skills. Gross is an independent journalist who specializes in environmental and public health, ecology, and conservation.

"Why Pesticides Could Be the Biggest Risk Posed by Corporate Agriculture," by Liza Gross, The American Prospect, www.prospect.org, August 26, 2016. Reprinted by permission.

As you read, consider the following questions:

1. According to this article, how does lowered IQ affect earnings later in life?
2. What chemicals in addition to pesticides does Gross say almost all US children have in their bodies?
3. What are some ways kids who live in agricultural communities are exposed to pesticides, according to Gross?

The latest statistics from the U.S. Department of Agriculture reveal that Americans' appetite for locally grown, organic food is growing. Consumers want to know where their food comes from and what's in it. Most polls show that the vast majority of Americans also support mandatory labels for genetically modified organisms, or GMOs. Nearly half of Americans think scientists have found risks associated with eating GM foods even though they haven't, according to a recent survey by the University of Pennsylvania's Annenberg Public Policy Center. "People don't know very much about the science, and they don't know that GMOs have been in the food supply for 20 years," says William Hallman, who ran the survey. "They just know they don't like it."

Last month, after years of contentious debate, President Obama signed legislation requiring the first national GMO labeling standard. (Labeling advocates aren't happy with the law because it lets companies choose whether to use a simple text label or a smartphone-accessible code to disclose GM ingredients.) But what's lost in the debates over imaginary risks from GMOs is the real threat posed by the way our food is produced.

U.S. farmers apply more than a billion pounds of pesticides to conventionally grown crops every year. It's no surprise that chemicals designed to kill living things that farmers consider pests can also harm us. There is mounting evidence that conventional agriculture's reliance on pesticides places agricultural communities, and especially their children, at risk for serious health problems.

Last month, University of California, Berkeley researchers reported that seven-year-olds scored lower on cognitive tests if their mothers were pregnant when high applications of organophosphates and other pesticides were applied to crops near their homes. On average, these children had lower IQs. They also scored lower on verbal comprehension tests.

The study, published in *Environmental Health Perspectives*, adds to a growing body of research which indicates that people who live and work in agricultural communities face increased risk for asthma, neurodegenerative diseases, cancer, and other chronic conditions related to pesticide exposure. Their children are more likely to have birth defects, cognitive difficulties, childhood cancers, lower IQs, and other developmental problems.

Much of what's known about how pesticides harm young brains has come from the UC Berkeley group, led by Brenda Eskenazi, a professor of maternal and child health and epidemiology. Through the Center for the Health Assessment of Mothers and Children of Salinas, or CHAMACOS, Eskenazi's team has been tracking families living in one of California's most productive agricultural regions to understand how pesticides affect kids' growth, health, and development.

Many families who live in farm communities around the country earn low wages. Clear evidence links childhood poverty to poor cognitive development and school performance. The Berkeley team suspected that pesticides could exacerbate these effects, but no one had investigated it before.

Not surprisingly, they reported in another study published earlier this year that children whose mothers lived near the highest pesticide applications and earned wages at or below the poverty level scored two points lower on verbal comprehension, working memory, and IQ tests. Those living in poor neighborhoods performed even worse, scoring roughly four points lower on the cognitive tests.

I asked Robert Gunier, an exposure assessment expert for the CHAMACOS project, whether these results have implications for urban kids living in low-income housing, where exterminators routinely spray insecticides to control cockroaches and other pests. "I can't say for sure without doing a study," he told me, "but based on this data I would say that higher metabolite levels in children who are either living in poverty or living in a poor neighborhood will likely have a larger effect."

Losing a few IQ points may not seem like a big deal. But lower IQs in the general population mean that many communities will see more children who need special education and lack the skills for independent living. Many studies have tied lower IQ to lower wages and lifetime earnings. "The easiest way to quantify the impact of lowered IQ in children is that a one-point reduction in IQ amounts to a $15,000 reduction in lifetime earnings," says Bruce Lanphear, an environmental health professor at Simon Fraser University in British Columbia who specializes in environmental brain poisons like lead and pesticides.

Four in five U.S. children are exposed to organophosphate pesticides, mostly from food. (Though several studies have also linked organophosphate exposure in pregnant women and children to residential insecticide use in urban areas, where indoor pest control is common.) In addition to pesticides, almost all children also carry levels of lead, mercury, the plastics additive bisphenol A, flame retardants, and dozens of other untested chemicals in their bodies.

Two years ago, Lanphear co-produced an educational video to help the public understand how exposure to even small doses of these environmental contaminants at critical windows of brain development can have far-ranging consequences. Little shifts in children's IQ scores have a big impact on the number of children who are challenged or gifted. Most of us have IQs between 85 and 115 and about six million children are considered challenged, with IQs below 70, while another six million are gifted, with IQs over 130.

A 2006 *Neurotoxicology* study found that exposure to a contaminant like lead, which causes a five-point drop in IQ, would lead to a 57 percent increase in challenged kids, from six million to 9.4 million children, and a corresponding decrease in gifted kids, from six million to 2.4 million children. Flame retardant exposures compound that effect, as do any number of other chemicals, including pesticides.

Lanphear and other environmental health experts worry that widespread exposure to these chemicals has contributed to the rising incidence of learning and behavioral problems in children, which jumped 17 percent between 1997 and 2008. Last month, he joined 46 other experts in a call to reduce exposures to chemicals that can harm the young brain. "On average, it costs twice as much in the United States to educate a child who has a learning disability as it costs for a child who does not," they argued.

They called organophosphate pesticides a "prime example" of toxic chemicals that can harm the developing brain. For kids who live in farm communities, it's hard to avoid pesticides. They can be exposed to volatile chemicals that drift from fields that are too close to their classrooms or homes and cling to toys or settle in dust. They can also be exposed to the chemicals through their diets or from hugging a parent whose clothing carries residues.

Biomonitoring surveys from the Centers for Disease Control and Prevention have found evidence that Americans who eat conventional fruits and vegetables are exposed to pesticides. Consumers can reduce these levels by choosing produce from organic farms, which often control pests with compounds like copper and sulfur that don't drift offsite and cause neurological harm like organophosphates and other synthetic pesticides can.

Last year, the federal government awarded 23 states $8 million in grants to encourage families in the Supplemental Nutrition Assistance Program to use their benefits at farmers markets, where organic produce can be cheaper. Public health experts say people who can't afford organic produce still need the nutritional benefits of conventional fruits and vegetables and can wash produce under running water to remove most pesticide residues.

Rather than worrying about unsubstantiated risks from GMOs, Americans should worry about the real risks pesticides pose for people in the communities that feed the nation. Consumers tend not to get as worked up about pesticide risks to farmworkers as they do about GMOs. That's because most people worry primarily about what they perceive as personal risks and tend not to think much about societal impacts, says Hallman, who led the Annenberg GMO survey. When Hallman asked people why they buy organic foods, most cited health as the primary reason (though evidence that organic food is more nutritional than conventionally grown food is also lacking), and environment second. It's natural for consumers to worry about their own health when it comes to pesticides, but the people who harvest our food, and especially their children, face far greater risks than the rest of us. Pregnant women in the CHAMACOS study had levels 40 percent higher than a national sample of women of childbearing age.

Yet his polls also show that even people who say they disapprove of GM foods would support using GM technology to reduce pesticide use. (Many anti-GMO respondents also said they'd embrace GM grass they didn't have to mow as much.)

So far, most GM plants designed to reduce pesticide use have "Bt" genes from bacteria that produce insecticides in the plants to fight pests that feed on them. The advent of Bt corn and cotton has led to a substantial reduction in insecticide use, scientists with the U.S. Geological Survey reported in May, but insects are evolving resistance to these plants, just as they do to insecticides. Since pesticides applied at lower rates could still harm the environment or public health if they're more toxic or prone to linger in the air, the USGS scientists couldn't say whether their use improved safety.

But even if they did, the vast majority of fruits and vegetables aren't modified to resist pests, so the people who pick them would still be exposed. Instead of engineering plants to produce pesticides, some researchers are trying to boost their innate defenses against pathogens, just as vaccinations protect us against measles and flu. But this work is just beginning.

Ultimately, growing crops without sacrificing the health of the farmworkers that Americans depend on to feed their families will require a massive overhaul of current farming practices. As a first step, farmers should phase out pesticides that scientists know or have good reason to suspect will harm young children. Over the long term, they must transition to less-toxic pesticides made from naturally occurring substances in bacteria, plants, and animals, and create healthy habitats around fields that attract birds and other natural insect predators.

The U.S. government has spent billions to subsidize industrial producers of pesticide-intensive corn, soybeans, and a handful of other crops that wind up as ingredients in processed junk foods, but only a fraction of that amount to support fruit and vegetable farms. Instead, American tax dollars should be used to help farmers adopt sustainable practices that protect agricultural workers and the communities they live in, while making healthy fruits and vegetables affordable for everyone.

> *"Globally, demands for an alternative food system must be made by a democratic food public that shares citizenship on a basis other than that of the nation-state."*

Democracy Demands that Control of the Food System Be in the Hands of the Citizens

Alana Mann

In this text, we've read many views—some of them scientific, others quite passionate—about how our food is or should be grown and distributed. As we saw in a previous chapter, in the viewpoint about Cuba, the sort of government and economic system a nation has can have many, and often unintended, consequences for its food production systems. In the following viewpoint, Alana Mann argues that our food choices are a political statement and that democracy requires that people, not large, multinational corporations, have control over their food. Mann is senior lecturer of media communications, international relations, and global studies at Sydney University in Australia.

As you read, consider the following questions:

1. What does Mann mean by "food citizenship"?
2. How, drawing on John Dewey, does Mann describe democratic publics?
3. What are some of the ways Mann suggests citizens can bring change in their communities and nations?

Calls for food democracy, which date back to the sustainable agriculture movement of the 1980s, have become more common with the increasing concentration of power in the global industrial food regime.

The current regime is inherently undemocratic. The intervention of democratic food publics—based on their shared experiences of the adverse effects of global foodways—is essential to transform a broken system.

This political project depends on recognition that this is a global public problem and that its solutions depend on new conceptions of citizenship.

Global regime requires citizens, not consumers

Corporate control of the global seed sector is one symptom of an undemocratic food system that favours transnational agribusinesses. Ten companies account for 55% of the seed market. Several dominate value chains from seed to supermarket shelf.

An endless array of processed, packaged and scentless products confronts us as consuming subjects, not citizens. We are forced to rely on the expert knowledge of food manufacturers, labellers and processors in our dietary choices.

In response, eaters concerned with "food from nowhere," as Josè Bovè puts it, aspire to recreate authentic relationships built on trust between growers and consumers. Shortening food supply chains—by buying directly from producers or opting for Fair Trade products—may bring us closer to this goal.

In respecting local foodshed boundaries by buying at farmers' markets, we express our dissatisfaction with corporate control through what Michele Micheletti calls "political consumerism." But individual action cannot counter the overpowering influences of liberalised markets and their impacts on rural livelihoods in a global economy.

While consumers' local micro-encounters may represent important attempts at communal autonomy, they do not address inequalities within and between communities. Privileged groups find it easier to participate. It is not simply that marginalised people lack the means to participate in farmers' markets and buy Fair Trade or organic produce; they have limited input into these initiatives.

For one of the industrial food regime's fiercest US critics, farmer-activist Wendell Berry, the revitalisation of local food economies is the strongest counter to a system that puts profit before human health, culture and the environment.

Organising alternatives

Sites of resistance from Vermont in the US to Larzac in France reflect the desire to protect local lifestyles and livelihoods. Food cooperatives such as Nueva Segovia in Nicaragua and Mondragon in Spain, urban land committees in Venezuela and the Greening of Detroit provide models of community control of resources and participatory democracy.

Alternative food networks and community-supported agriculture aim to reconnect producers and consumers in local human, cultural and land ecologies. These schemes are increasing alongside civic food networks in which eaters practise "food citizenship": food-related behaviours that help develop a democratic food system.

Multi-stakeholder structures such as food policy councils in the US and Canada and associations for the maintenance of smallholder agriculture (AMAPs) in Europe support many of these innovative models. They are creating and connecting new spaces for democratic debate on environmental sustainability, social justice and economic viability.

Rather than seeking to maximise local consumption, critics of industrial agriculture should concentrate on creating democratic food publics to tackle structural problems with the food system. These include food deserts in poor neighbourhoods and rules that grant corporations property rights over seeds.

When the industrial food system is perceived as a public problem, rather than a personal responsibility, a greater diversity of experiences and perspectives can contribute to solutions. The vision of localised food systems is not sufficient to bring about food democracy for the one billion people most affected by poverty and hunger. This is particularly so when the intellectual property, free trade and investment agreements that govern food and agriculture transcend national borders.

Drawing on John Dewey, democratic publics are comprised of individuals who recognise the adverse impacts of the activities of others and act collectively to demand the state protect their interests. Globally, demands for an alternative food system must be made by a democratic food public that shares citizenship on a basis other than that of the nation-state.

Uniting in a fight for food sovereignty

One such public is the transnational peoples' movement La Via Campesina. It represents small-scale producers, pastoralists, migrant workers, fisherfolk, landless peasants and indigenous peoples in 70 countries across the global north and south. For more than 20 years, members have embodied an "agrarian" citizenship that goes beyond class-based notions of political representation.

La Via Campesina provides a model of rural action based on common interests in the different struggles against policies that impact negatively on farmers worldwide. These impacts include low crop and livestock prices, exploitative temporary farm labour, distorting subsidies and the disappearance of family farms.

The question of food is fundamentally social. Who should provide food and how? Whose livelihoods should be protected?

La Via Campesina's concept of food sovereignty, the right of peoples to define their own food and agriculture policies, is a proposal for radical social transformation to make food systems more democratic. It has evolved from a catch-cry opposing trade liberalisation to a concept adopted by broader constituencies. Among these are food democracy advocates in the global north who share the view that the corporate food system actively contributes to global hunger, poverty and malnutrition.

The campaign for food sovereignty spans many issues including gender inequality, land reform, genetic modification, intellectual property, biodiversity, urban agriculture and labour migration. It has emerged as a political project that talks to power at venues including the United Nations Committee on World Food Security.

Hundreds of members of La Via Campesina and like-minded organisations met recently in a very different forum in Sèlinguè, a village in Mali, West Africa. The resulting Declaration of the International Forum of Agroecology presents the peoples' alternative to conventional industrial agriculture and the destructive elements of international trade.

It states that traditional methods of food production such as intercropping, mobile pastoralism and composting play an integral role in creating equitable, sustainable and healthy food systems, as opposed to monocultures and biotech solutions.

The meeting declared:

> Agroecology is the answer to how to transform and repair our material reality in a food system and rural world that has been devastated by industrial food production and its so-called Green and Blue Revolutions … [it is] a key form of resistance to an economic system that puts profit before life.

A revolution of a different colour, agroecology is based on farmers' local innovation and peer-to-peer information sharing and diàlogo de saberes (ways of knowing through dialogue). It seeks to return power to communities, to:

… put the control of seeds, biodiversity, land and territories, waters, knowledge, culture and the commons in the hands of people who feed the world.

Relocating control of food production and distribution to growers and eaters rather than corporations requires the mobilisation of publics of citizens committed to resolving the public problem that is our food system. The building of coalitions between consumer-oriented initiatives and the more radical food sovereignty movement is essential to develop a long-term constructive agenda for widespread change.

While practising political consumerism and strengthening local food economies are important, only the emergence of democratic food publics based on new notions of citizenship can achieve such change.

Periodical and Internet Sources Bibliography

The following articles have been selected to supplement the diverse views presented in this chapter.

Wyatt Bechtel, "What Is Food Morality?" Agweb.com, January 8, 2017. http://www.agweb.com/article/what-is-food-morality -wyatt-bechtel.

Judith Benz-Schwarzburg and Arianna Ferrari, "The Problem with Super-Muscly Pigs: Technologies to genetically engineer sentient animals for meat production raise questions about the human-animal relationship, Slate, June 3, 2016. http://www.slate.com /articles/technology/future_tense/2016/06/the_ethical_ problems_with_super_muscly_pigs.html.

Josh Harkinson, "Slaughter-Free Milk Is Great for Cows, but Not the Environment," *Mother Jones*, July 21, 2014. http://www .motherjones.com/environment/2014/07/downside-no-kill -dairies.

John Ikerd, "Why Corporate Industrial Agriculture Has Made Life in Rural American a Lot Worse," Alternet, March 24, 2015. http:// www.alternet.org/economy/why-corporate-industrial -agriculture-has-made-quality-rural-life-america-lot-worse.

Frederick Kaufman, "Genetically Monetized Food," Slate, December 20, 2012. http://www.slate.com/articles/life/food/2012/12/plant_ patent_law_why_overhauling_it_will_do_more_to_help_the_ food_movement.html.

Tom Philpott, "How Factory Farms Play Chicken with Antibiotics: The Inside Story of One Company Confronting Its Role in Creating Superbugs," *Mother Jones*, May/June 2016.

Amanda Radke, "How Can We Show Consumers Our Morality and Integrity?" Beefmagazine.com, June 30, 2014. http://www .beefmagazine.com/blog/how-can-we-show-consumers-our -morality-and-integrity.

Paul Solotaroff, "In the Belly of the Beast: Animal Cruelty Is the Price We Pay for Cheap Meat," *Rolling Stone*, December 10, 2013. http://www.rollingstone.com/feature/belly-beast-meat-factory -farms-animal-activists.

Rhys Southan, "Execution at Happy Farm: Which world would be better: one in which all meat is grown in a lab or one which still contains humanely farmed animals?" Aeon, August 24, 2016. https://aeon.co/essays/what-makes-a-better-world-lab-grown -meat-or-humane-farming.

Leigh Vincola, "Revisiting Ethics in Sustainable Agriculture," PermacultureNews.org, April 24, 2015. http://permaculturenews .org/2015/04/24/revisiting-ethics-in-sustainable-agriculture.

For Further Discussion

Chapter 1

1. Steve Savage says that many changes in agriculture and agricultural policy were made as a result of the environmental movement of the 1970s and the establishment of the Environmental Protection Agency. He specifically mentions the development of "no-till" farming and newer types of pesticides. Do you think these changes have made a positive difference? Why or why not?

2. Zareen Pervez Bharucha points out that while many people in the world are suffering from hunger, others are suffering the health effects of obesity. Both of these groups suffer from malnutrition—not getting enough of the right kinds of nutrients and not getting a proper balance of nutrients. Simply increasing crop yields will not solve this problem, she say. Do you think her suggestions would remedy that problem? If not, have you seen other articles in this book that offer better suggestions?

3. In his article, Brian Halweil points out that gaps between crop yields of organic and conventionally farmed produce are largest in industrialized nations. Why evidence does he use to support this claim? Do you think he makes a good case for why an "integrated approach" might be the best solution?

Chapter 2

1. Bill Hewitt connects the fact that the United States produces an enormous amount of corn to the political situation. Do you think that reducing subsidies and eliminating ethanol requirements would help reduce

global warming? At the end of his article, he also suggests that individuals eat less meat and less food sweetened with corn syrup. Do you think that would make a significant difference? Why or why not?

2. Some suggest that farming needs to be more heavily regulated by the government. Yet we just heard from Bill Hewitt that politics are at least in part responsible for the overproduction of corn that leads to many environmental problems. Is there a difference between government regulatory agencies, such as the EPA, and the Congress, which passes laws about subsides and ethanol requirements? How might a government that supports agricultural policies that damage the environment also regulate that industry?

3. Miguel Altieri raises concerns about Cuba's agricultural and economical future. In what other ways can political world changes affect agriculture and food systems? How could such problems be mitigated?

Chapter 3

1. Olga Bonfiglio explains the reasoning behind the industrialization of the food system but says that the benefits do not outweigh the risks. What examples does she give of this? Do you think that greater support of local food systems, as Bonfiglio recommends, would make a significant difference in the problems she brings up?

2. According to Carrie Mess, it is a real challenge for small farmers to keep their operations small. What challenges does she list? Does her argument makes sense to you? Can you think of ways farmers could address the problems she mentions without expanding the size of their farms?

3. Jaclyn Moyer, a small farmer in California, says that she is unable to make a living farming, yet Logsdon says not only does he and his family manage to do it, others

can as well. What do you think is the difference in their two situations? Why might Logsdon be more hopeful about the future of small, organic farming than is Moyer? Logsdon mentioned that the government needed to provide "a level playing field" for family farms to compete with industrial farms. Do you think this would make a difference for farmers like Moyer? Why or why not?

Chapter 4

1. Much of the argument that factory farming is immoral rests on the claim that it harms people and the environment. Yet most experts say that the damages are not as severe as opponents suggest—especially when it comes to genetically modified crops, one of the most hotly contested aspects of modern agriculture. Does the potential for GMOs to reduce other harms of corporate farming weaken the arguments of those who say corporate farming is morally unjustifiable? Why or why not?

2. Nadia Prupis says that the scientists who vouch for the safety of GMOs can't be trusted because they have financial ties to the industry that profits from the technology. Do you think it is possible to be objective about an issue when all or part of your incomes comes from a company with a stake in that issue? Why or why not? On the other hand, Layla Katiraee says that much of the science cited in objection to GMOs is either faulty or deliberately deceptive. Which argument is more convincing to you? Katiraee's or Prupis's? Why?

3. Why does Alana Mann see food as undemocratic? Imagine a world with food sovereignty: What would "democratic food" look like? What would need to happen in the world to achieve this?

Organizations to Contact

The editors have compiled the following list of organizations concerned with the issues debated in this book. The descriptions are derived from materials provided by the organizations. All have publications or information available for interested readers. The list was compiled on the date of publication of the present volume; the information provided here may change. Be aware that many organizations take several weeks or longer to respond to inquiries, so allow as much time as possible.

Bioversity International
Via dei Tre Denari, 472/a
00054 Maccarese (Fiumicino), Italy
bioversity@cgiar.org
website: http://www.bioversityinternational.org

Bioversity International delivers scientific evidence, management practices, and policy options to safeguard agricultural and tree biodiversity to attain sustainable global food and nutrition security. It offers news, details on policy initiatives, and opportunities for fellowships.

Center for Food Safety
660 Pennsylvania Avenue SE, #302
Washington, DC 20003
(202) 547-9359
office@centerforfoodsafety.org
website: http://www.centerforfoodsafety.org

The Center for Food Safety (CFS) is a national nonprofit public interest and environmental advocacy organization working to protect human health and the environment by curbing the use of harmful food production technologies and by promoting organic and other forms of sustainable agriculture. CFS also educates consumers concerning the definition of organic food and products.

CFS uses legal actions, groundbreaking scientific and policy reports, books and other educational materials, market pressure, and grass roots campaigns through its True Food Network. CFS's successful legal cases collectively represent a landmark body of case law on food and agricultural issues.

The Cornucopia Institute
PO Box 126
Cornucopia, WI 54827
(608) 625-2000
cultivate@cornucopia.org
website: https://www.cornucopia.org

The Cornucopia Institute sponsors educational activities that support the ecological principles and economic wisdom that underlies sustainable and organic agriculture. Through research and investigations, the Cornucopia Institute provides needed information to consumers, family farmers, and the media.

Food and Agriculture Organization of the United Nations
Viale delle Terme di Caracalla
00153 Rome, Italy
FAO-HQ@fao.org
website: http://www.fao.org/home/en

The Food and Agriculture Organization of the United Nations (FAO) leads international efforts to defeat hunger by working to create a world free of hunger and malnutrition where food and agriculture contribute to improving the living standards of all, especially the poorest, in an economically, socially, and environmentally sustainable manner.

Genetic Literacy Project
8 West 126th Street, Suite 3B119
New York, NY 10027
(410) 941-9374
info@geneticliteracyproject.org
website: https://www.geneticliteracyproject.org

The Genetic Literacy Project, a part of the Science Literacy Project, explores the intersection of DNA research and real world applications of genetics with the media and policy worlds in order to disentangle science from ideology. The commitment of the GLP is to promote public awareness and constructive discussion of genetics, biotechnology, evolution, and science literacy.

Institute for Agriculture and Trade Policy (IATP)
2105 First Avenue South
Minneapolis, MN 55404
(612) 870-0453
website: http://www.iatp.org

IATP works locally and globally at the intersection of policy and practice to ensure fair and sustainable food, farm, and trade systems.

International Federation of Organic Agriculture Movements (IFOAM)
1 Charles-de-Gaulle-Str. 5, 53113
Bonn, Germany
(503) 235-7532 (US phone)
D.Gould@ifoam.bio
website: http://www.ifoam.bio

IFOAM is an umbrella organization of groups supporting organic food and agriculture in 117 nations. It works to facilitate production and trade, promote sustainability in agriculture, and help build the capacity of leaders in the organic movement.

Organic Federation of Canada

12-4475, Grand boulevard
Montreal, QC H4B 2X7
(514) 488-6192
info@organicfederation.ca
website: http://organicfederation.ca

The Organic Federation of Canada brings together all the key players in Canada's organic industry to ensure excellent standards and regulations that stimulate the growth of Canada's organic sector, which is good for the environment, the consumer, family farms, and rural communities. It offers information to help consumers identify organic products.

Rodale Institute

611 Siegfriedale Road
Kutztown, PA 19530-9320
(610) 683-1400
info@rodaleinstitute.org
website: http://rodaleinstitute.org

The Rodale Institute works with individual growers at every level—from those who just have a few backyard containers to farmers growing on thousands of acres. It trains new farmers interested in organic agriculture, supports conventional farmers in transition, and works to ensure that all organic farmers are as efficient and economically viable as possible. In addition, the Rodale Institute works with cities and organizations to create viable opportunities for the next generation of organic farmers.

**United States Department of Agriculture/
Agricultural Law Information Partnership**
National Agricultural Library
10301 Baltimore Avenue
Beltsville, MD 20705
(301) 504-5755
website: https://www.nal.usda.gov/aglaw/agricultural
-law-information-partnership

The Agricultural Law Information Partnership is a new collaboration between the National Agricultural Library, the National Agricultural Law Center (NALC), and the Center for Agriculture and Food Systems (CAFS) at Vermont Law School. The partnership supports the dissemination of agricultural and food law information to consumers, researchers, and legal professionals. Agricultural law is defined broadly to include land-based agriculture, food and fiber production and systems, aquaculture, and energy issues.

Bibliography of Books

Barry Estabrook, *Pig Tales: An Omnivore's Quest for Sustainable Meat.* New York, NY: Norton, 2015.

Sonia Faruqi, *Project Animal Farm: An Accidental Journey into the Secret World of Farming and the Truth About Our Food.* New York, NY: Pegasus, 2016.

Philip H. Howard, *Concentration and Power in the Food System: Who Controls What We Eat?* London, UK: Bloomsbury Academic, 2016.

Frederick Kaufman, *Bet the Farm: How Food Stopped Being Food.* New York, NY: Wiley, 2012.

Gary Kleppel and John Ikerd, *The Emergent Agriculture: Farming, Sustainability, and the Return of the Local Economy.* Gabriola Island, British Columbia: New Society Publishers, 2014.

Jayson Lusk, *The Food Police: A Well-Fed Manifesto About the Politics of Your Plate.* New York, NY: Crown Forum, 2013.

Henry Miller and Gregory Conko, *The Frankenfood Myth: How Protest and Politics Threaten the Biotech Revolution.* Westport, CT: Praeger, 2004.

Marion Nestle, *Food Politics: How the Food Industry Influences Nutrition and Health.* Berkeley, CA: University of California Press, 2013.

Brian K. *Obach, Organic Struggle: The Movement for Sustainable Agriculture in the United States.* Cambridge, MA: MIT Press, 2015.

Raj Patel, *Stuffed and Starved: The Hidden Battle for the World Food System.* Brooklyn, NY: Melville House, 2012.

Robert Paarlberg, *Food Politics: What Everyone Needs to Know.* New York, NY: Oxford University Press, 2013.

Michael Pollan, *The Omnivore's Dilemma: A Natural History of Four Meals.* New York, NY: Penguin, 2007.

Peter Pringle, *From Mendel to Monsanto: The Promises and Perils of the Biotech Harvest.* New York, NY: Simon and Schuster, 2003.

Marie-Monique Robin, *The World According to Monsanto.* New York, NY: The New Press, 2012.

Joel Saladin, *Folks, This Ain't Normal: A Farmer's Advice for Happier Hens, Healthier People, and a Better World.* New York, NY: Center Street, 2011.

Vendano Shiva, ed., *Seed Sovereignty, Food Security: Women in the Vanguard of the Fight Against GMOs and Corporate Agriculture.* Berkeley, CA: North Atlantic Books, 2016.

Jeffrey M. Smith, *Seeds of Deception: Exposing Industry and Government Lies About the Safety of the Genetically Engineered Foods You're Eating.* Portland, ME: Yes! Books, 2003.

Paul B. Thompson, *From Field to Fork: Food Ethics for Everyone.* New York, NY: Oxford University Press, 2015.

Tony Weis, *The Global Food Economy: The Battle for the Future of Farming.* Black Point, Nova Scotia: Fernwood Publishing, 2007.

Bill Winders, *The Politics of Food Supply: US Agricultural Policy in the World Economy.* New Haven, CT: Yale University Press, 2009.

Index